IN THE BEGINNING WAS I

A novel of mystery and self-discovery

Written
By
Mahmoud Farra

Dedication

To my muse. To the one who rose from my dreams to submerge me in the ocean of her fantasies. She confuses the mirrors and dazzles them. She has no face—yet she has a thousand faces, and one.

An iris with an enigmatic fragrance. Is it a Damascene rose, or is it a lily? Or perhaps an orchid… or jasmine? The rainbow borrowed its colors from her.

It learned from her how to paint the sky and color the soul. It learned from her how to be—and how not to be. She gives birth to me at sunrise and sings to me. But after sunset, she swallows me whole. And still, I long to be her prey to feel the crack of my bones in her arms. She is not just one she is all women. She hid herself within all my mermaids. She is Isabelle and Louise.

She is Rose and Lamees.

To the one who has become my wife.

Table of Contents

Dedication 1

Chapter One 4

Chapter Two 10

Chapter Three 24

Chapter Four 40

Chapter Five 82

Chapter Seven 104

Chapter Eight 124

Chapter Nine 138

Chapter Ten 147

Chapter Eleven 151

Chapter Twelve 160

Chapter Thirteen 174

Chapter Fourteen 191

Chapter Fifteen 196

Chapter Sixteen 210

Chapter Seventeen 239

Chapter Eighteen 254

Chapter Nineteen 277

Chapter Twenty-One 290

Chapter Twenty-Two 296
Chapter Twenty-Three 303
Chapter Twenty-Four 309

Chapter One

If there is any mystery surrounding our existence, dreams are among the most powerful manifestations of this great mystery. Dreams are our second life, our indispensable life. It all begins when we close our eyes.

The noise in the bunkers and cells gradually gets louder, and as soon as we fall asleep, the dream jinn emerge from their hiding places. They rush madly towards our deepest depths, towards the dungeons dug in the dark catacombs of our minds, towards the locked boxes of secrets buried in the convolutions of our brain.

The doors of the cells open, and the locks of the boxes break, releasing the demons of our repressed desires and forbidden selves and freeing our instincts from their constraints.

All laws of nature are violated; logic is lost as we fly, soar, and weave in the space of our selves.

In dreams, barriers disappear, the forbidden is no longer forbidden, and immorality is no longer immoral. Everything becomes permissible. It is a magical world where the mind is absent, replaced by instincts, passions, repressed desires, and deep fears.

When we begin to awaken, every demon returns to its cell, and every jinni locks itself in its box and closes in on itself. When we open our eyes, we have gathered the fragments that scattered throughout our daily lives and healed the cracks created in our souls by our social relationships. When we wake up, most of our dreams are lost; we remember only what nature has allowed us to remember. Meanwhile, our memory loses what our nerves cannot bear or comprehend, out of mercy for us and our mental health.

I gasped in fear. I felt my heart pounding. I opened my eyes and found myself panting in my bed.

"Calm down," said Louise, as she wiped the sweat from my face.

"What happened?"

"You were just dreaming."

"Oh my! What a disturbing dream! I don't know what's happening to me! It has been recurring frequently in the past week."

"Is it the same dream?"

"Yes, it's the same girl. I encounter her alone on the beach. I follow her, and suddenly I find myself in old Damascus neighborhoods. I find myself following her without control? I try to make her stop because I don't want her to continue because I know the place where she's going, and I know that place frightens me. Yet she always lures me to that same dark and frightening alley. I try not to enter it, but she forces me to follow her. As soon as I take my first step into the alley, darkness envelops me, and she disappears, leaving me alone. I wake up gasping in fear."

"What scares you? Is it the girl?" Louise asked sarcastically.

I laughed, adjusted my sitting position on the bed, and said, "Girls don't scare me. It's you who frightens me and stirs up terror."

"Don't joke. Tell me, do you think that woman is me?"

I said mockingly, "Why do you want to force yourself into my dreams? Must the woman be you?"

"So, there's another woman?"

"Do you know what time it is now? It's four in the morning, and people across California are sleeping. You're in my bed, naked in my arms, and despite all that, you're asking me if there's another woman? Does it really matter to you if you are that woman or that you have all this influence on me?"

"Yes, if she is the one you seek out and follow without control."

"But she always takes me to that horrible, desolate place. I tremble just thinking about that place."

"Do you think I'm taking you there? To that horrible, desolate place?"

I said, laughing, "You take me to worse places."

"Listen, let me make an appointment for you with my psychiatrist."

"I don't need him; frankly, I'm jealous of him. I think in the end you'll be captivated by him and marry him."

"Stop joking."

"I'm not joking. I don't understand why you insisted on visiting him and spending your money on him. If it's not love, what would you call it?"

"I call it trust in the doctor."

"Is he better at giving massages than I am?"

"Oh, Mamdouh, your humor is unbearable!"

"Is he better in bed?"

She moved away from me, half-angry, and turned her face to the other side of the bed.

"You're a moron. Go back to sleep. I was wrong to advise you to consult a doctor. All I want for you is to get rid of this nightmare."

I hugged her and said to her in an apologetic tone, with my fingers slipping towards her breasts and playing with them despite her resistance:

"I'm not used to talking to anyone about my private life, even if it's a doctor. Anyway, I don't think I need a doctor. I think it's homesickness."

Louise said, having surrendered and allowed my hands to do their task: "Why don't you take a vacation? When was the last time you went to Syria?"

"Since I came to the United States twenty years ago."

"I think it's time for you to go. You need to go."

"So you want to send me away and get rid of me?"

She wrapped her arms around my waist and rested her head on my chest:

"Perhaps you'd miss me a little and dream of me sitting on the sands of the ocean shore thinking of you."

"Do you think my departure will be beneficial?"

"Yes, I think it might benefit both of us."

"Tell me, Louise, do you enjoy sex with your doctor more than with me?"

"Damn you."

Chapter Two

I rang the doorbell, and a beautiful young woman who barely looked fifteen years old opened the door. She looked at me with surprise, then smiled hesitantly and whispered cautiously.

"Uncle?"

"How did you recognize me?" I said, laughing in astonishment. She didn't answer but shouted at the top of her voice, "Mom, hurry, it's Uncle Mamdouh!"

It was a moving reunion.

Hanan is my little and only sister. She's still beautiful. Her forty years hadn't changed her appearance much, except for adding some lines to her face.

She asked me in her sarcastic style that tended toward reproach: "Why did you cut yourself off from us all this time in America? You could have visited us from time to time."

"I was busy."

"Too busy to see us? You haven't even met Zeina since her birth; you've only seen her during some moments when you both happened to be online at the same time."

I was silent for a moment. I had expected such a question, and although I had intended to answer, something prevented me. How could I explain to her what was difficult for me to explain even to myself?

I told her, "Tomorrow, I'll tell you. I'm tired now. Let me breathe in the scent of Damascus and enjoy it."

The scent of the place filled my being a distinctive fragrance that inhabits your nose in most Damascus houses, a mixture of the scent of air, earth, Arabic ghee, and soap a fragrance I had longed for.

When the car that brought me from the airport reached the entrance of Damascus city at the Bab Sharqi area, I felt a hidden joy and familiarity with the place, as if I had passed by here just yesterday. Despite its noisy appearance, Damascus is distinguished by how it creeps quietly and slowly toward time, indifferent to the developments around it, like someone lazy who doesn't want to wake up from their dreams and step outside their walls. Perhaps history has exhausted it, or maybe it has begun to feel old age. The scenes hadn't changed much from when I left them: the old Bab Sharqi area still welcomes you at the entrance of the city, and the streets are still crowded with people, fruit and vegetable carts, vendors of cassette tapes of folk and Bedouin singers, ice cream vendors on the sidewalk, and carts pulled by horses or donkeys sneaking into some neighborhoods of the city, either in negligence of the law or in collusion with it.

Hanan said as if remembering something:

"But first, tell me how you knew about the box?"

"What box?"

"Didn't you come because of the box?"

"What box? I don't know what you're talking about."

"Strange... Isn't it a strange coincidence that you come after twenty years at the same time when we need you here. If not for the box, may I ask what suddenly brought you back to us today after such a long absence?"

"It's the dream."

"What dream?"

"A week ago, I saw a strange and beautiful dream, and it urged me to return."

My words aroused Hanan's curiosity, and she said: "Really? Tell me about it."

"It's an ordinary dream. we were young and we were playing in the neighborhood near the house you, me, and some of the neighbors' children."

Hanan and Zeina followed my conversation with passion and complete silence. Then, when I stopped talking, my sister stared into my eyes and asked in confusion, "And then?"

"Then what? Nothing. That was the dream."

I didn't wait long before she hit me, as was her habit, with a pillow on my head, amid Zeina's astonishment and amusement.

"My God! I've forgotten your tricks; it's as if you've never traveled."

I said, laughing: "Why are you angry?"

"You go away for twenty years, and we worry about you for twenty years. You don't ask about us all this time, and then you claim you're only coming back because you dreamed that we were playing in the neighborhood?!"

"Would you like to know the real reason?"

She said with interest: "Of course."

"One of the saints came to me in my sleep while he was chewing gum and told me, 'Go visit your sister because she misses you, so I came to you as fast as possible.'"

"Did you hear this, Zeina? This is your uncle, gray-haired but still foolish. Don't listen to what he says."

"I really did miss you."

"It's hard for me to believe that. Did you really come back for us?" she asked, looking at me with a look full of question marks.

"Listen, what I miss most right now is a cup of coffee from your hands."

She gestured to Zeina, who jumped from her place: "Get up, Zeina, and make a cup of coffee for your uncle."

"No, you make the coffee, and you, Zeina, come sit by my side." Zeina approached me, looking at me shyly, then sat near me. "Do you know that you resemble your grandmother?"

"Yes, everyone says that."

"Tell me, how did you recognize me immediately?"

"Your pictures fill the walls of my room. Come and look."

She took me to her room, which had a wall covered with many hanging pictures. She pointed to a picture of all of us together my father, mother, me, and my sister. That was the last picture taken of us before my father's death. I was eighteen then, and Hanan was fifteen.

Zeina spoke enthusiastically as she pulled photo albums from one of her dresser drawers. She resembled Hanan and my mother.

We started looking at the pictures during coffee, and I had a large share in them.

Zeina said, "You and my mother had a good relationship. You were together in many places and events."

"Your uncle was more my friend than my big brother, despite his foolishness that you notice only a small part of, he was my window to the world."

"So you're admitting that I'm the reason you're smart."

She asked me suddenly while looking at the pictures:

"Are you married?"

I laughed and said, "You know I'm not."

"Why aren't you married?"

"I don't like this topic now. Let's talk about it later."

I saw Hanan putting one of the albums aside.

"What's this album?"

"You'll see it later," she said, putting it away.

"What's in it?"

"Perhaps you shouldn't see it now. It's an old memory."

"Don't tease me. Give it to me. I have a strong desire to reclaim all memories."

"All of them?" Hanan asked with a sarcastic, mocking tone.

She handed me the album and watched me as I flipped through it.

The hot coffee almost burned my throat as I looked at the first picture. As if the running train of the forgotten past had suddenly stopped, a twenty-year-old girl stepped out, smiling and steadily approaching me. She extended her hand as she shyly said, "Hi, I'm Lamees."

"That's Lamees," I said in astonishment.

Hanan didn't comment but continued to observe the different expressions on my face as I silently reviewed the pictures.

"You didn't ask about her." She said.

"About whom?" I asked, my eyes fixed on Lamees, who kept approaching and getting closer to me, her hair flying in the air. She extended her hand to me with that smile engraved in my memory: "Hello, I'm Lamees."

"About whom?" Hanan said sarcastically. "Lamees, of course. You didn't ask me about her news. Well, I'll tell you anyway."

Lamees refused marriage for a long time, even after graduating from university. After a while, she disappeared, locked herself at home, and didn't go out anymore. Many things changed in her. She immersed herself in studying and dedicated herself completely to it. She gained weight, and she isolated herself from everyone, even from me, despite my love for her and her love for me.

Her joy disappeared, and the brightness and radiance left her eyes. Two years later, with her family's insistence, she got married.

(Lamees looked at me and said with a sad look in her eyes: I can only belong to one man, to you.)

But her marriage didn't last more than a few months, and she was divorced. She remarried again, but she divorced again shortly afterward.

(Lamees said in a desperate voice, "I will never get my orgasm except from you. I don't know how I will live in this body after you. Your fingerprints and the traces of your lips are in every corner of it. How can I remove your tattoo from my heart? They say removing a tattoo is a painful operation.)

"Then suddenly, the entire course of her life changed. I'm sure you won't recognize her. I saw her once in the market after years of disconnection. She smiled at me from afar and waved to me. She was completely different, another person I had no connection with, not the Lamees you knew. One of her friends once confided in me that she still occasionally talks passionately about you and couldn't love anyone but you."

I shifted uncomfortably in my seat and tried to appear uninterested as I asked her:

"Does she work?"

"Yes, she's a university professor. She teaches French in the Faculty of Arts."

"And how is she doing?"

"All I know about her now is that she has changed a lot. She is not the Lamees I once knew, neither in appearance nor in essence. She has completely changed. I personally no longer know her."

"Alright, let's leave this topic for later. Now tell me the story of the box."

Hanan smiled mischievously and said, "Well, if that's what you want, they found a buried box in the middle of the house garden."

"What house?" I interrupted

"Our house," she said angrily, "the family house."

"Do you mean the house where Abu Jassim and Abu Anwar live?"

"Yes, that's it—our family home."

The family house! The stolen one. The house of my childhood! The place where my mother and I lived for less than a year. This was in 1958, during a time when a sectarian war broke out in Lebanon. My father was working in Beirut, at a women's beauty salon he owned. He feared for our safety amid the chaos of the war. He sent my mother and me to Damascus so we could be safe. Though my father was born in Damascus in a district called Bab Srijeh, he didn't have a house there, so there was no place for us to live.

Before we left, he gave my mother all his savings to buy a house, and she did exactly that.

She purchased a spacious two-story house in one of Damascus's suburbs, specifically in the Eastern Ghouta area, surrounded by land filled with trees. However, my father chose to remain in Beirut for reasons he did not disclose, despite my mother's urging and the dangerous situation there.

After one year and the end of the conflict, we returned to Beirut and left our house. A military man I knew by the name of Abu Anwar rented it. Abu Anwar took advantage of his position and our absence from the country and sublet the ground floor for his benefit to a man known as Abu Jassim, while he settled on the upper floor.

"And what's in the box?"

No one knows. They haven't opened it yet. They're waiting for your arrival to open it. The mukhtar Abu Hamza has often asked about you or your address. Abu Anwar also called to inquire about you. He was very polite on the phone, unlike usual. He asked how my husband, my daughter, and I were doing and if we needed anything, as he knows my husband travels frequently. Do you think there's a treasure in the box? They all think so.

"Who do you mean by 'all'?"

"The mukhtar Abu Hamza, Abu Jassim, and Abu Anwar. No one else. They have kept it secret and haven't told anyone anything, waiting for your arrival to open it. They said they won't open it unless you're present."

"Oh, that's strange. Why would they wait for me? Why didn't they open it in your presence? After all, you're also the owner's daughter.

"They want you specifically. I don't know why. Perhaps out of respect for you. They were very polite, as I told you."

I laughed sarcastically and said, "No, no, there's something unnatural here. Why would they wait for my presence to open the box if there's supposed to be a treasure in it?"

"So what do you think? Could they have already opened the box and found out what's inside?"

"Of course, they opened it. What would prevent them from opening it and dividing its contents?"

"If what you're saying is true, why did they inform us of its existence in the first place?"

"I don't know."

"You're scaring me. Why do they want you then?"

I thought for a moment and said, "You should dismiss the idea that they want me for something good or beneficial to us. Our father, as you know, died without owning any wealth or money, only the house they've taken over. And he, like us, didn't live in the house because we were living in Lebanon, where he worked."

Zeina interrupted me: "Why did my grandfather stay in Lebanon all his life?"

"Frankly, I don't know the reason, though he was fascinated with Damascus. He spoke about it with great admiration and affection. However, I only recall him returning to it once, the time he died there. I remember a day in Beirut when it was Eid, and he was talking enthusiastically and with longing about the Eid rituals in Damascus. He was missing his sister Maryam there, so I took advantage of his enthusiasm and longing to convince him to accompany us to spend the Eid days in Damascus. I remember how his facial features changed as he refused, using his work as an excuse. Yet, under persistent urging from me and my mother, he reluctantly agreed. However, on the day of travel, he changed his mind and didn't accompany us, leaving us to go without him."

"Could he have secretly buried his wealth in the ground inside this box?" my sister asked.

"If there were wealth, they would have seized it as I told you, without telling anyone, especially us."

I continued, in a sarcastic tone that was also serious: "Perhaps they found something in the box that would bring us misfortune."

"Oh my God," my sister cried, "like what?"

"Perhaps a corpse, weapons, or drugs. Or maybe they want to pin some charge on us so they can completely take over the house. I don't trust them. Perhaps the mukhtar has an idea. I trust only him. Anyway, I'm tired now. I'm content with what I've learned so far today. I'm considering going to my apartment, but I don't know if it's still habitable."

"Don't worry, I'll send someone to clean it now so it will be ready. But you can stay with us as long as you wish."

"Listen, soak the chickpeas now because our breakfast tomorrow must be a feast of hummus with pine nuts and genuine local ghee."

Chapter Three

I couldn't sleep that night despite my fatigue. The story of the box occupied my mind throughout the night.

My father did indeed own a box a long time ago, but it wasn't important, and no one ever showed any interest in it; then it disappeared, and no one ever mentioned it again. The last time I saw my father's box was when he was holding it in the taxi throughout our journey from Beirut to Damascus. It was a medium-sized wooden box that could be carried by hand. My father didn't let go of it for a single moment during the entire trip.

He was silent, sometimes resting his head on it and closing his eyes. He never allowed me to help him carry it. I didn't know that would be his final journey to Damascus. I blamed myself for his death because he had gone there reluctantly and against his will. I wanted to travel to America to study, and he had to accompany me to the American Embassy in Damascus or else I wouldn't get the visa. I had tried in vain to get it from Beirut, as Syrians were required to obtain their visas from Syria.

My father was quiet by nature and would often sit alone at home. He didn't have friends, and he would sit silently, not exchanging conversation with us. He would spend hours in deep thought and then doze off in his place on the couch in front of the television.

My mother was always busy with her neighbors, friends, and markets, never caring much about him. He never complained; on the contrary, he would find excuses for her to go out and leave him alone. I always sensed that he was exhausted, worn out, and lacking vitality. We weren't on good terms, he and I.

He was indifferent to life; nothing excited him. I never remember him being happy about anything. He was detached from worldly matters, and that used to hurt and anger me.

When I think about it today, I feel that contradiction in his life. His work with women all day long in the beauty salon required someone cheerful and talkative, not a quiet, silent, and depressed person. Perhaps for this reason, his work declined in the last period, or perhaps, on the contrary, the poor work situation caused him depression. In any case, he was skilled in his work, as my mother, acquaintances, and his clients witnessed.

Although he could barely read or write in Arabic, he occasionally surprised us with French phrases and sentences, which he pronounced with a Parisian accent. We would laugh at his unexpected language skills. The strange thing is that I never thought to ask how he learned those phrases with a Parisian accent, as if it were something natural that we were accustomed to. When he went to work, he always wore a formal suit with a tie even in the heat of summer, and carried an expensive leather briefcase that appeared to be filled with papers and documents but in reality contained makeup and nail polish tools. He used them when visiting some of his preferred clients in their homes. I rarely saw him in simple clothes. Even when he wanted to go to the vegetable market he would wear a suit and tie. I once asked my mother about this sarcastically, whispering, "Who does he think he is?" She smiled and shook her head, and said: "It's Rose."

"Who's Rose?!!"

He kept a distinctive silk tie in his closet, featuring a beautifully crafted eagle in gold and blue colors. Although the tie was old, he wore it on special occasions. It seemed a bit unusual, as it didn't conform to the prevailing fashion trends.

"It's a gift from Rose!" my mother said.

"Who is Rose?" I asked, but I didn't dare to ask him directly.

However, the answer came spontaneously from him during one of the evenings spent with some friends at home when he was talking extensively about Damascus, its neighborhoods and customs, and how people wore the Damascene Kumbaz and the tarbush.

"Have you ever dressed like them, Dad?" I asked.

"Of course! I'm a son of Bab Srijeh, after all, which is an ancient neighborhood in Damascus. But I was the first to wear suits and ties in the neighborhood," he said, feeling proud.

"I've been wearing French suits since I was fifteen years old."

"How can a son of a poor neighborhood, as you say, wear French suits?"

My father was silent, and stroked his head a little, then returned to speak in a voice filled with sorrow and longing:

"It's Rose."

I burst out, eager to know, "Who is Rose?"

My father smiled shyly and tried to evade answering, but under the pressure of my insistence, or perhaps because he felt the need to reveal this secret, he said in a quiet voice:

"Rose was a French girl who traveled to Damascus to visit her fiancé, a French officer. She fell in love with the city and decided to settle there. Rose opened a beauty salon for women, offering services such as hair cutting, styling, facials, and nail polishing for both hands and feet. Her salon was among the first in the area at that time."

"And what was your relationship with her?"

"I was fourteen years old, I lived with my siblings in a small house in Bab Srijeh. My parents had died when I was young, so I didn't know them. Our older sister, Maryam, took care of us. She worked as a seamstress to support us and made sure I could attend school to learn reading and writing, as well as to memorize the Quran under the guidance of some mosque sheikhs. Sometimes I would help her sell local mulberries during spring, carrying them in small baskets and wandering with them in the upscale neighborhoods and wealthy areas of Damascus."

"One day, I was calling out for mulberries in the Abu Rummaneh area, which is one of the wealthy areas with beautiful villas surrounded by fruit gardens, especially pomegranates. I stood at the entrance of one of the new buildings and shouted at the top of my voice, advertising my goods, when a foreign girl came out of one of the ground-floor apartments. She was very beautiful and very kind, around twenty years old. She spoke to me in French, but of course I didn't understand. She asked me by gesture what I had, so I offered her the baskets. She tasted a mulberry, liked its taste, and asked me to come in. The apartment was actually a beauty salon, filled with French and Damascene women from the upper class. I felt embarrassed as they surrounded me, tasting the mulberries and laughing. I stood there, looking at the ground in shyness, having never seen such beautiful women up close. I was fascinated by the place and its many mirrors and by the women and their beauty. It was a momentous event for me, and I didn't know it would completely change the course of my life."

"She spoke to me in French, saying, "I am Rose, Rose." She repeated this several times until I understood it by ear.

"She asked for my name. I replied, "Ahmed." She smiled and gave me much more than the expected price for the mulberries. Then she requested that I bring her another quantity the following week. So I did. I started bringing her mulberries weekly, and each time she would let me into the salon and get me a cold drink. She would put the mulberries on small plates and offer them to her clients. During this time, I would sit cross-legged in one corner, drinking juice and watching her cut hair or polish nails. She would sing and laugh, and sometimes she would forget my presence, and I would remind her that I needed to leave and take my money.

"But eventually, the mulberry season ended.

"I was disappointed and confused about what to do. I no longer had a reason to visit the salon. I didn't mind that I lost her money; I was saddened that I would never enter the salon or see her again. At that time, the cactus fruit season had begun, so I found an opportunity to reconnect with her.

"A few weeks later, I went to her, arriving a bit late and carrying a basket of cactus fruit. I entered the salon, It was empty of clients. She was alone and busy polishing her nails. She seemed to be in a hurry. She got up smiling when she saw me and welcomed me, then took a curious look at the contents of the basket, and before she could ask what it was, she quickly reached out and grabbed one, heedless of me. I tried to warn her, but she was quicker than I was to catch it. I promptly took it out of her hand, but it was too late. She backed away, terrified, and started screaming and waving her hands in the air, uttering incomprehensible words. I tried to apologize, but she was angrily turning her face away from me while feeling the thorns in her fingers. I quickly grabbed a pair of tweezers and asked her to sit in the barber's chair while I carefully and patiently removed the barbs from her hand. She calmed down a bit, and her frown disappeared. She took the tweezers from me and started removing the thorns herself. I stood watching as she worked. After a moment, she glanced at her watch and then looked at me, extended her foot, and handed me a bottle of nail polish, nodding toward her foot. I understood what she wanted. I had watched her do it repeatedly for her clients, so I started polishing her toenails with great care and caution, while she was busy removing the thorns from her fingers. I finished with the first foot. She scrutinized my work, and finally, she seemed pleased and extended her second foot.

When she finished removing the thorns, her smile returned. I peeled a few cactus fruits for her, and she cautiously tasted the first one, liked it, and took the rest of them. She kept looking admiringly at my nail-polishing work the whole time. We left the salon together, and as I was about to leave, she asked me to return the next morning for something.

Fate was waiting for me the next day to change the course of my life.

She asked me in French if I wanted to work with her in the salon. I agreed without hesitation and said, "I'll start immediately." She laughed and gave me a white garment and asked me to stand, watch, and help her clean the salon I observed her work each day and cleaned the salon afterward.

Every day after work, she would train me to polish the nails of her hands and feet, teach me how to handle nails and use the necessary tools like scissors and files. Our language consisted of signs and some French vocabulary that I was learning quickly. Despite everything, she never allowed me to touch any of her clients' nails. However, one day, a woman rushed in while Rose and her assistant Janine were busy. In that moment, she asked me to polish the woman's toenails while she took care of her fingernails. This was the first time I did real work. My work pleased that lady. It marked the beginning of my journey in this profession. One day, Rose looked at me and said something in French I didn't understand. She repeated it several times, pointing to my clothes, and then took me to a tailor and asked him to make me a suitable suit matching the salon's reputation. And that's how I got the suit and abandoned the kumbaz.

I asked inquisitively: "What happened to her? And where is she now?"

My father was silent and said without much thought: "I don't know. I later quit the salon and settled in Beirut. She went her own way. She might have returned to France."

Like all women, this conversation about Rose didn't please my mother, but despite that, she listened with interest, and that bothered him and made him hesitant to continue.

I said with regret, "Why did you leave the salon? Why did you go to Beirut? Where is Rose now?" He didn't answer my questions, and the answers remained ambiguous.

And this was the first and last time my father talked about Rose.

He didn't utter a single word to me during our journey to Damascus. He wasn't the type to show his emotions, and he never cared about anything. I never saw him angry about anything that would deserve anger.

His silence in the car worried me, so I assumed he was sad about my travel because he was completely against it. He knew about my impulsiveness and feared for my nature.

"You're still immature, and I know you're weak with women."

"How long will you keep treating me like a child?"

"You lack experience with women. I know them well, I work with them all the time. They will devour you alive, especially in America".

Now with sadness, I remember how he looked at me throughout the journey, giving me advice about travel and study, then falling silent for a while, then remembering something and giving me another lesson about how to deal with people or how to save money.

When we arrived in Damascus and stepped out of the taxi near the entrance to (Ahmediyyah Souq) We were tired. I was carrying our luggage and hurrying to reach my aunt's house, where we would stay during our time in Damascus. But my father stood in his place for a while, not moving, looking in a specific direction while still carrying the box.

He said:

"Do you know the place where you were born and raised? It's a neighborhood there called Bab Srijeh."

There was longing and joy mixed with some fear in his words. I told him nervously:

"Let's go to my aunt's house now; we can return to Bab Srijeh later when there is plenty of time. The most important thing right now is to finish the visa paperwork."

I don't think my father heard a word of what I said, because he was not the father I knew. He ignored what I said and started walking in slow, steady steps toward Bab Srijeh as if there was an enchanted voice calling him and pulling him toward it. I followed him reluctantly, carrying the travel bag with frustration, until we reached the entrance to the Bab Srijeh neighborhood.

He stood silently for a moment, gazing at the neighboring shops and peering into the long-covered souq as if he were searching for something. He was breathing with difficulty.

"Are you looking for someone?" I asked, a hint of impatience in my voice.

He didn't answer me. Instead, he remained standing with caution and alertness in his eyes, and a hint of sadness in his gaze. I rationalized this as a natural response to returning home after a long absence.

He didn't seem to notice my presence. I respected his feelings and didn't speak. I put the bag on the ground and waited for him to indicate something to me.

After a while, he moved forward slowly, hugging the box tightly in his arms. That was the first time I entered this neighborhood and this souq. The small shops were lined up on both sides, and everything spoke of history. The dominant smell of the affects every visitor. We walked into the long souq, the sun had already set, and the market was lit with electric lights. I was walking behind him, feeling constrained, but I didn't want to spoil his reunion with his neighborhood.

He was not walking randomly but was heading steadily toward a specific place. We reached a junction that led to a narrow, deserted alley. He stopped at the intersection and began looking with frightened eyes into the dark alley that seemed almost endless. He kept staring into the darkness of the alley with fear in his eyes. His breathing quickened and became irregular, and sweat began to pour down his face. Grabbing my hand firmly, he pressed it as if seeking help and said, "Come on, let's get away." Without looking back, he quickly moved away from the alley, pulling me behind him.

When we left the souq for the main street, he was more relaxed and returned to his usual self.

Two days later, he died. And his death was a mystery.

We stayed with my aunt Maryam, "Umm Hassan." He was happy to meet her after years of absence, and she was also very touched and happy with his arrival. That night, we were tired, my father and I, but despite that, when we wanted to go to sleep, my aunt insisted that he stay with her for something, saying there was an old message from someone he knew and he should see it.

I left them and went to bed. They were talking about some topic and whispering as if it were a secret that no one should know. He didn't stay long with her; he returned to the room after a short while, but I don't think he slept that night, or at least not immediately, because I woke up several times, and he was always near the window, lost in thought, thinking about something.

During that visit to Damascus, my father never left my side. We went to the American Embassy together, where I was approved for the visa. Afterward, we had time to visit the rest of the family and relatives. He also took me on several tours of the old souqs in Damascus, and he was like a small child, amazed by everything, as he had memories tied to every street we passed through.

That was a special period in the relationship between my father and me. He was unusually cheerful, with vitality radiating from his eyes, talking enthusiastically about everything. He took me and introduced me to relatives I didn't know. He spent considerable time searching for people and found some, although most had left no trace. Finally, the embassy procedures were completed, and I got the visa. While we were preparing to return to Beirut and finish our business, he carried the box, which I had completely forgotten about. He told me he would go alone to care of something special, and then we would set off on the return journey. But he didn't return that night. I searched a lot for him in all the places he might be, but found no trace of him.

The next day, someone from a hospital contacted us to inform us that he was in the hospital and that he had died.

We later learned that his body was found after the dawn prayer in Bab Srijeh, in the same place he had taken me before. He was sitting on a small chair, with his back and head leaning against the wall. He had passed away wearing the tie with the golden eagle, and there was a slight smile on his face.

It was a great shock to me and all of us. After that, I gave up traveling to America. My mother and I decided, under my aunt's insistence, to return to Syria. And so we left Beirut for good and returned to settle in Damascus.

Abu Anwar refused to hand over the house to us, claiming it was for security reasons. So we were forced to buy a small apartment.

My mother, Hanan, and I lived in the apartment. Then, after two years, Hanan got married and left the house. After a while, my mother died, and I remained alone in the apartment.

Chapter Four

In the morning, I woke up disturbed by my sister's voice telling me that Mukhtar Abu Hamza had come asking about me and was waiting for me in the salon.

"Get up, Mamdouh, the man is here."

"Can't he wait till after breakfast??"

I sighed in frustration. I hadn't gotten enough sleep that night, and all my efforts to return to sleep were unsuccessful, so I got up reluctantly.

As soon as Abu Hamza saw me, he rushed toward me, embracing me and extending his good wishes for my safe return, as if we were ever close friends.

He was in his seventies yet still exhibited a remarkable amount of energy and vitality.

People loved him despite his pretense of not liking anyone. Still, his generosity and eagerness to help others contradicted his claims of wanting people to leave him alone. You would find him present at every occasion: weddings, funerals, celebrations, and festivals. He's everywhere. His life could be described as a collection of contradictions. For instance, he fulfills his prayer duties, yet this doesn't stop him from heading to his farm for lunch with a few glasses of arak after Friday prayers.

"My son," he would justify, "God is forgiving and merciful. He knows what's in my heart and that I wish nothing but good for people, so why should He punish me for a little grape juice?" This is how he used to respond to those who dared to question him.

People were united in their love for him. However, they differed on other issues—some praised his generosity and aid to those in need, while others questioned his piety and accused him of a dissolute lifestyle. But no one dared to confront him directly, fearing his sharp tongue. In any case, Abu Hamza had an inexplicable affection for me. We didn't know each other well, apart from some business dealings where I approached him like any other citizen. He considered himself an old friend of my father's and claimed they had grown up in the same neighborhood.

We shared coffee together, and he inquired about my well-being while gently teasing me for my lengthy absence. Hanan asked him about Lamees.

I should mention that Lamees is the mukhtar's daughter. Perhaps that explains his fondness for me? In any case, I don't believe he knew about my relationship with Lamees. I suspect he only knew that we had been together at the university.

"Fine, fine," he said, clearly trying to dodge the question. Then he turned toward me: "So tell me, how did you find America?"

Hanan wasn't satisfied with his evasiveness and pressed him: "Is she in Damascus, or is she traveling?"

Abu Hamza stammered, "She's in Damascus." Then he continued to me, "Do they have mukhtars in America like we do here?"

But Hanan would not let him off the hook and kept matching his evasiveness with her persistence:

"Then why won't she answer my calls? I've been trying to reach her since yesterday, but she wouldn't pick up."

"I don't know why she's not answering," he said, clearly on the verge of losing his temper. Then he collected himself: "Frankly, Umm Zeina, I prefer not to discuss her. I know you're close friends. Perhaps we can talk about her another time, but not today and not in front of Mr. Mamdouh. There's no need to trouble him with family matters."

"On the contrary," I interjected with curiosity, "we'd like to know how she's doing. What's her news?"

The mukhtar surrendered uncomfortably, realizing he was cornered with nowhere to retreat. "We don't stay in much contact," he admitted. "I honestly don't know whether she's well or not. We had a falling-out some time ago, and she stopped calling me. I can't figure her out anymore—that girl is driving me out of my mind. All her siblings have married and settled down, all except her. She's stubborn and defiant, and I do not influence her whatsoever. She lives independently and makes her own decisions. Do you remember what she was like when you knew her at university, Mr. Mamdouh?"

I wondered if he knew about our relationship. I shot Hanan a glance, but she looked away. I turned back to the mukhtar, who was waiting for my response.

"Of course, I remember her; she was a brilliant student."

"That's precisely the problem—her studies. They've consumed her entire life and continue to do so. But I'm not referring to her academic pursuits. I'm talking about how she's changed as a person. She used to be modest and gentle, but university transformed her completely. She no longer confides in me or shares what's in her heart. She's become confrontational and dismissive of everyone's counsel."

I could feel him sweating, and he was eager to leave.

"I warned you—let's drop this subject, Umm Zeina." I've already burdened Mr. Mamdouh enough with my rambling. Let's not speak of Lamees anymore. Discussing her troubles makes my heart race and sends my blood pressure soaring. If she weren't your dear friend, I would never allow myself to talk about such family matters.

"Mr. Mamdouh, I'm sure your sister has mentioned the box to you. The construction workers found it while digging in the garden behind your family home the property where Abu Jassim lives.

"But why were they excavating the garden in the first place? That area lies beyond the main structure and was never included in the rental agreement."

They have now enclosed the entire garden within the residential compound?

"Do they have the right to do that? Isn't it illegal? How can they make such changes without my explicit consent?"

"Listen carefully, Mr. Mamdouh. Abu Anwar wields considerable influence and can justify almost any action under security concerns. Don't challenge him on such matters while the situation remains volatile and the country unsettled. Once stability returns, you can pursue your rightful claims against them. For now, avoid stirring up unnecessary trouble for yourself."

"So, what's our connection to this box?"

"The box belongs to you."

"To me?"

"Yes, and I'll say no more about it. We need you to be present tomorrow when we examine the contents."

"If you're telling me it's mine, that suggests you've already looked inside so why do you need me there?"

"No, we haven't opened it yet."

"Why not?"

"You'll understand why tomorrow. I can't elaborate now, or I'll only deepen the mystery. Your best course is to come to my office tomorrow afternoon, and from there, we'll proceed to Abu Jassim's house."

I arrived at the mukhtar's office right on time. A military vehicle was parked outside. Only Abu Anwar was there, dressed in military fatigues adorned with lieutenant's insignia. He cradled a coffee cup in one hand while thoughtfully stroking the tip of his thick mustache with the other.

"Here's Mr. Mamdouh—punctual as always," the mukhtar announced, then turned to Abu Anwar with a knowing smile. "I told you he would have adopted their habits by now—precisely on time, unlike us locals who treat time so casually."

"Actually," I replied with subtle irony, "the lieutenant has outdone me—he arrived before I did, which clearly demonstrates that he too respects time."

"Hello, Mr. Mamdouh. Thank God for your safe return. How are you?"

"I'm fine, but don't understand what the mukhtar asked me about. Are you planning to evacuate the house?"

The lieutenant recoiled visibly. He shifted uneasily in his seat and shot the mukhtar a look of reproach and anger, while the mukhtar, equally taken aback, stood behind his desk, stammering: "Who told you that? You've clearly misunderstood. The lieutenant has no intention of vacating the house at present."

"There are pressing security considerations requiring us to maintain the house for now," the lieutenant said curtly. "But that's not why we brought you here. We want to show you something we discovered in the garden. Let's leave immediately." He stood abruptly and gestured for me to follow.

The mukhtar interjected: "I'll follow in my car."

Outside, he pointed to the driver rushing toward us, shouting and cursing loudly for no apparent reason, then brusquely motioned for me to get in the car.

"I'd prefer riding with the mukhtar if it doesn't trouble you," I said diplomatically. "We wouldn't want him driving alone."

"As you wish," the lieutenant replied tersely, then gave sharp orders to his driver before leaving.

The mukhtar approached me with a reproachful expression: "May God have mercy on your father—try to let things proceed smoothly. Let's get in the car, though I'm afraid it's rather uncomfortable."

A wave of familiarity washed over me when I stood before the house. Though I had only lived here briefly during the Lebanese sectarian troubles of the 1958s, that time was enough to forge a meaningful connection with the place. I remember playing and finding joy in every corner of the house. It was a traditional Damascene residence with the character of a small estate.

A large, well-maintained garden separated the residence from the main street, stretching from the entrance to a two-story building where Abu Jassim occupied the ground floor. The garden had once been unfenced, but now a tall barrier shielded the residence from public view. Walking through the garden, I noticed a significant excavation in the ground.

"That's where they discovered the box," the mukhtar explained.

Umm Jasim greeted us at the entrance, pushing a wheelchair occupied by a man wearing dark glasses—clearly vision-impaired. He greeted, "Welcome, Mr. Mamdouh."

I recognized the voice immediately—Abu Jassim's.

I hadn't known about his blindness, and I felt embarrassed that no one had informed me. "Please, come in," he said with genuine warmth.

"What befell him? Has he lost his sight?" I murmured.

"Diabetes," the mukhtar whispered back, guiding me forward into the house.

We entered a spacious parlor whose simple furnishings conveyed comfortable yet unpretentious circumstances.

The lieutenant was already there. As we arrived, he stood abruptly and said, "Fetch the box. Let's conclude this business."

"Perhaps some coffee first?" Abu Jassim suggested, attempting to ease the tension. "Please, be seated." He turned toward Umm Jasim with forced cheer: "Umm Jasim, would you prepare coffee for our guests?"

"We have no time for coffee. Bring the box immediately," the lieutenant snapped.

"Of course, of course—the box," the mukhtar hurriedly agreed. "The lieutenant has pressing obligations."

The woman stepped back momentarily, returning with a wooden box that she placed on the table in front of me. The moment I laid eyes on it, I recognized it immediately. It was unmistakably my father's wooden box. I lifted it gently and examined it closely: "This belonged to my father."

Abu Anwar confirmed, "We're aware it was your father's. We uncovered it during the excavation work in the garden."

"Then I'll claim it now."

"Not until we ascertain its contents," the lieutenant interjected firmly.

I observed that the lock had been tampered with.

"But it has already been opened."

"Indeed—we broke the lock. We did not know its ownership until after we'd examined it."

"Then what further need is there? You've seen what's inside."

"Not entirely," Abu Anwar replied thoughtfully. "Are you familiar with the contents?"

"No, I'm not."

"Ok then, examine the pouch inside and reveal what lies within."

The way he spoke sent a chill down my spine. My mind raced with possibilities, wondering what secrets it might hold. I leaned forward and carefully lifted the lid. I could feel everyone's eyes boring into me, watching my every movement. The box's interior was lined with red velvet, revealing a white envelope and a small black velvet pouch. As I placed my hand inside, everyone instinctively stepped back, as if the box might contain something explosive. Their behavior struck me as strange.

I retrieved the envelope and found that it had already been opened, with a single sheet of paper inside.

"It's a letter addressed to you from your father," Abu Anwar announced. "Read it aloud."

"To Mamdouh, my beloved son."

I faltered, the words catching in my throat. Suddenly, my father's face appeared before me, his presence reaching across time through these written words. "My beloved son"—never before had my father expressed such tender sentiment, and I was transported back to our always-strained relationship, which left little room for emotional intimacy.

My youth was defined by foolishness and poor judgment. The fragile thread of understanding between us nearly snapped completely. I loved him deeply, without question, yet we never discovered ways to express it. I constantly challenged his choices and contradictions while he patiently endured my criticism.

I recalled my frequent outbursts against him how I would reproach his preference for solitude and withdrawal. He would retreat to his room silently, closing the door behind him. I never allowed myself the vulnerability to express my affection, nor did I create space for him to reveal his own.

He had been like a bowl of sweets resting on a familiar shelf—always present, I was used to its presence that I stopped truly seeing it. I found the bowl had vanished when I finally needed it, leaving nothing but an empty shelf behind.

"Now that you've discovered the box, I honestly cannot say whether I hoped you would find it or whether I would have preferred to take these memories to my grave. But since you're reading these words, it suggests you're fated to continue the search as I did. Because no one else can do it. My blood courses through your veins, your dreams are the continuation of mine, and your memory preserves mine. You are my past and my future, just as I am yours. When I look upon you, I see myself reflected, and should you look deeply within yourself, you will also find me there.

Truth does not reside outside ourselves; it's inside us. Yet, some of us are not ready to embrace it. Perhaps I was among those unprepared souls. I was so close to grasping it, but it was destined to slip through my fingers—maybe so it might reach you instead. Blessed is the one whom nature selects to unveil its mysteries, for nothing in the universe surpasses such beauty.

it is that magnificent radiance of which I, regrettably, caught merely a fleeting glimpse; yet even that fragment illuminated my entire existence and revealed how transcendent and wondrous the complete revelation would be.

Now that this quest has become your calling and sacred duty, I pray you find what I could not, and that it brings you the peace and serenity that eluded me."

Despite its vague nature, the message conveyed a clear sense of paternal devotion, lifting the heavy burden of guilt from my shoulders and replacing it with endless love.

The mukhtar placed a gentle hand on my shoulder. "May God grant your father eternal rest—he was a righteous man, truly blessed."

"Enough sentiment," Abu Anwar interjected, shifting restlessly in his chair. "Let's conclude this business. Now then—confess."

"Confess to what?" I asked, genuinely confused.

"To the truth. I deal only in facts." He adjusted his position, deliberately crossing one leg over the other.

"What truth are you referring to?"

"The truth your father hinted at in his letter. This treasure you're supposedly seeking."

I had to suppress an almost irrepressible urge to laugh. Collecting myself, I replied: "I'm afraid I know nothing of any treasure, Lieutenant. Perhaps whatever you're referring to remains among the box's other contents, which, as you can see, constitutes my inheritance. I fail to see how any of this concerns your authority."

"And what exactly is that object in the box?" he demanded, his voice adopting a menacing tone.

I said with mounting irritation: "What business is it of yours? What business is it of any of you? This belongs to me alone. You had no right to open the box in the first place. Now that you have, and you know it's mine, I'm taking it and leaving."

But the lieutenant blocked me: "You're not taking anything until I understand what's inside."

"The box is open!" I shouted, my anger flaring. "Here, take it, examine it!"

"Hey be careful. You will address me with the proper respect. You clearly don't understand who you're dealing with."

"Mr. Mamdouh intends no disrespect," the mukhtar quickly interjected, positioning himself between Abu Anwar and me before facing me with a meaningful wink.

"Please, remain calm, Mr. Mamdouh. The lieutenant's interest in the box's contents isn't driven by idle curiosity—there's something genuinely disturbing about what lies within."

Growing exasperated, I seized the box and thrust it directly into Abu Anwar's hands. "Is this what you're so desperate to examine? Then by all means, take it."

The lieutenant recoiled as though I had handed him a live serpent, crying out in terror as he hurled the box across the room. The woman fled instantly, vanishing from sight. The mukhtar scrambled backward until his spine pressed against the wall. They all scattered like startled birds, leaving me alone in the center of the room.

An oppressive silence settled in, thick with anticipation. Then Abu Jassim struggled to his feet—he had fallen from his chair during the sudden exodus. Disoriented, he reached around until his fingers found another seat. Once settled, he called for his wife and demanded an explanation for the chaos.

The black velvet pouch had spilled from the overturned box, and every eye in the room fixed upon it with unmistakable dread.

"What in God's name is wrong with all of you?" I demanded, instinctively backing away from the pouch as if their terror had proven contagious. Their reactions suggested that the thing might detonate at any moment.

Gradually, everyone crept back toward the box, maintaining their distance.

The mukhtar spoke hushed: "There's something profoundly unnatural about that object. Every person who has touched it has suffered acute respiratory distress and nearly lost consciousness."

I stared at the pouch in disbelief. It seemed to be nothing more than an innocuous black velvet pouch secured with a matching drawstring. Yet something solid lay within.

The mukhtar continued: "Abu Anwar is convinced that, according to your father's letter, you alone possess the ability to examine its contents safely."

"Proceed, go ahead," the lieutenant commanded, his voice tight with nervous energy. "Take the pouch and reveal what lies within."

I ignored his authoritative tone—I needed no orders, being far more intrigued than any of them. I extended my hand with deliberate caution. The moment my fingers touched it, I drew in a sharp breath as if pure oxygen were cascading through every cell of my lungs, saturating them completely yet leaving me without any urge to exhale.

Waves of euphoria and transcendent pleasure surged through my entire being. I closed my eyes and beheld towering peaks, profound valleys, flowing rivers, vast seas, pristine lakes, drifting clouds, and infinite skies. A deep serenity enveloped me, as if the entire cosmos had become my domain. Yet I remained fully conscious—everyone continued to observe me with expressions of amazement.

"What's happening to him?" Abu Jassim inquired, scanning the room with his sightless gaze.

"He's made contact with the object," the woman responded, her eyes fixed on the mysterious pouch.

With newfound tranquility, I picked up the pouch from the floor and sat in the nearest chair.

"Proceed—open it," Abu Anwar commanded with a military brusqueness.

"Patience, Lieutenant," the mukhtar interjected. "Allow the man a moment to collect himself."

Their words hardly registered. I remained captivated by the exquisite sensation, suspended in a state somewhere between trance and ecstasy. I loosened the drawstring with measured movements and reached inside, withdrawing the concealed object.

"What in heaven's name is that?" the lieutenant exclaimed. "Can this be real?"

"What is it? What is it? Describe what you've found!" Abu Jassim demanded urgently.

"It appears to be a camera," the mukhtar commented, uncertainly. "Is that correct?"

Indeed, it was precisely that—an antique camera from the 1940s, complete with an attached flash unit. Despite its age, the device remained pristine, its surfaces gleaming as if freshly manufactured. I rotated the camera gently in my hands while the others leaned in closer.

"What kind of camera is this?" Abu Jassim persisted.

"I haven't the faintest idea," I admitted, continuing my examination. "My father never once mentioned such an object, nor do I know how he acquired it."

I began to scrutinize every detail with increasing fascination. On the surface, it seemed to be a standard camera without any immediately noticeable distinguishing features. Given the precision of its craftsmanship and the remarkable quality of its lens, it would likely have been costly in its time.

"It's simply an ordinary camera," I announced to the group.

Then why would your father go to such extraordinary lengths to hide it in that box and bury it as if it were treasure?

"I'm afraid I don't know."

The mukhtar asked, "I wonder—does it still contain film? Is the device functional? Perhaps you could attempt to take a photograph."

I tried to access the film compartment, but it remained stubbornly sealed. Locating what I assumed was the shutter release, I pressed it deliberately. Instantly, a tremendous flash erupted—a brilliant burst of radiance that flooded the entire room with such intensity that it temporarily blinded us all. The light was accompanied by a piercing feminine scream that seemed to tear through our souls with primordial terror.

We all cried out in shock and pain—myself included—while the camera slipped from my startled grip to the floor. For several disorienting seconds, the world descended into complete darkness. When our vision gradually returned, we stared at one another in bewildered silence.

Abu Anwar was the first to speak: "Is everyone unharmed? Did you all hear that woman's cry? Umm Jasim, was that your voice?"

"Certainly not," she replied with evident distress. "I heard the scream just as clearly as you did. But who could it have been?"

"I have no idea, but that voice was chilling," Abu Anwar muttered. "And what kind of illumination was that? Could any camera flash possibly generate such overwhelming brightness?"

Meanwhile, Abu Jassim stayed motionless, as if his sightless gaze had somehow locked onto me. We all shifted our attention to him.

"Are you feeling well?" Umm Jasim asked with increasing concern.

"I'm... uncertain," he responded slowly, massaging his eyes. Then he turned toward me with surprising precision: "Mr. Mamdouh, are you perhaps wearing a blue shirt with vertical stripes?"

Everyone's eyes instantly turned to scrutinize my outfit, specifically, my blue striped shirt, with looks of utter amazement.

"Yes, that's correct," I confirmed, my voice barely concealing my amazement. "How could you possibly know that?"

"For one extraordinary moment, I saw you with perfect clarity—as though my sight had been miraculously restored. Then the vision vanished as suddenly as it had appeared. What in heaven's name just occurred?"

"The camera's flash mechanism activated," I simply explained.

"Could you... Would you be willing to try again?" Abu Jassim pleaded; his voice heavy with desperate hope.

The camera lay still on the floor, making occasional mechanical buzzing sounds. I picked it up and tried to trigger another flash by repeatedly pressing the button. Nothing happened. Eventually, even the intermittent buzzing faded into silence.

"Please," Abu Jassim implored, "allow me to handle it myself."

"No!" Abu Anwar intervened sharply. "Don't touch that device—it could prove dangerous."

"I care nothing for potential risks," Abu Jassim declared with fierce determination. "Give it to me. Perhaps if I operate it personally, my vision might return permanently."

With great reluctance and utmost caution, I handed the camera to his outstretched hands. The moment it settled in his grip, a palpable hush enveloped the room. We all watched Abu Jassim intently, half-expecting him to collapse under the weight of whatever mystical power the device might hold.

"Are you experiencing any strange sensations?" the lieutenant inquired anxiously. "Any unusual effects?"

"Nothing whatsoever," Abu Jassim replied with evident disappointment. "I feel perfectly normal." He explored the camera's surface methodically, searching for controls, pressing various buttons in seemingly random combinations. Still, nothing occurred.

After several futile attempts, he paused and spoke with quiet conviction: "I give you my solemn word—I truly did see Mr. Mamdouh. His shirt is indeed blue with stripes, is it not?"

The mukhtar intervened: "Allow me to attempt it." He carefully accepted the camera, rotating it methodically in his hands while exploring its surface with his fingertips and testing various controls—all to no avail.

Once the lieutenant convinced himself that any immediate danger had subsided, his boldness returned. He seized the camera and examined it contemptuously.

"So, this is your grand mystery?" he sneered with undisguised derision. "We've wasted precious time on absolute nonsense. Here—take your treasure." He threw it dismissively at my feet.

"My apologies for disappointing your expectations," I replied with matching sarcasm as I retrieved the device. "You must have been anticipating buried fortune."

Abu Anwar's laughter carried a cruel edge: "Where would that wretched barber have acquired any treasure worth finding?"

"That's quite enough, Abu Anwar," Abu Jassim interjected firmly.

"We should depart," the mukhtar suggested urgently, attempting to guide me toward the exit.

I carefully returned the camera to its velvet-lined refuge, secured the box, and moved toward the doorway.

Had I walked out at that crucial moment, my narrative would have concluded there—we would all have dispersed to our separate lives, and I might have relegated the camera to some forgotten corner among discarded household items. But fate demanded its predetermined conclusion. The lieutenant was compelled to deliver his fateful command: "Stop. Leave the camera here."

"What possible use could you have for it?" the mukhtar demanded.

"I'm having it sent to a photographic laboratory for professional analysis. There may be exposed film inside—we need to determine what images it contains before returning it to him."

"Very well, if you insist," the mukhtar conceded, surrendering the camera before practically dragging me from the premises as though fleeing an impending catastrophe.

During our drive to my sister's residence, I maintained complete silence while he shared his modest recollections of my father. He also resided in the Bab Srijeh quarter and would encounter my father during Quranic memorization sessions at the mosque.

"We weren't particularly intimate friends, you understand. He was somewhat my senior, but undeniably a righteous man. He possessed genuine ambition and harbored extraordinary dreams. Unlike the rest of us who chased after fleeting romantic diversions, he would speak of having someone special in mind—an exceptional woman, unlike any other, a girl without equal in this entire world. He remained perpetually hopeful, ever patient. May God grant him eternal peace. Your dear mother must have embodied his every aspiration; may her soul rest in paradise."

I absorbed his words in contemplative silence, embracing the now-empty box as my father had done during that long journey between Beirut and Damascus.

As I prepared to exit the vehicle, he offered his parting counsel: "Listen carefully, Mr. Mamdouh—don't allow today's unpleasantness to trouble you further. The lieutenant is chronically ill-tempered and vindictive. Dismiss him from your thoughts entirely. By the way, what are your plans for this evening?"

"Nothing special. I planned to visit my sister and then go to my apartment."

"Nonsense—you'll spend the evening at my countryside retreat. I maintain a farm in the Duma region that I believe you'll find quite agreeable. We'll share a proper dinner. Rest yourself now, and I'll pick you up at nine o'clock this evening."

I expressed my gratitude while trying to decline, but his insistence proved overwhelming, and I accepted reluctantly. Before leaving, he leaned close and whispered conspiratorially: "We'll enjoy some proper drinks—it promises to be a memorable night."

I managed a smile: "As you wish. Thank you "

"Prepare yourself for an evening of genuine celebration."

I found myself wondering if Lamees might be present.

Instead of going directly to my sister's house, I felt compelled to walk and sort through my turbulent thoughts. From the moment my fingers touched that mysterious camera, something fundamental shifted within me. My mind achieved an unusual clarity, and my earlier anger completely dissipated. I experienced unfamiliar emotions while Lamees's image dominated my consciousness with startling vividness.

I wandered extensively through the familiar streets, clutching the vacant box, questioning why memories of Lamees had suddenly reawakened such powerful feelings. Was this merely the influence of familiar surroundings? Did I truly miss her personally, or was I mourning the lost innocence of youth she represented? Could her unexpected return to my thoughts be connected to my recent dreams and discovering my father's hidden box?

The uncomfortable truth was that I had never genuinely forgotten her. I had been deceiving myself all these years, pretending I had moved beyond the woman who had captured my heart during our university days. I found myself wishing Louise were here, craving feminine companionship, and yearning for the comfort of a woman's embrace. Yet, even as I acknowledged this need, I felt tremendous guilt. I realized with shame that I only sought Louise when physical desire overtook me.

But something deeper within me raised a troubling question: "Is Louise truly the woman you desire now?"

The answer was devastating in my heart's deepest, most honest recesses. It wasn't Louise I wanted—it was Lamees who had suddenly taken over my every thought. Her memory had resurfaced to revive her image from the dusty corners of my mind, accompanied by waves of profound remorse.

Hanan had warned me that Lamees had changed dramatically, gaining weight and losing her former grace. The mukhtar described her as having become confrontational and bitter. I couldn't help but wonder about her current appearance; despite everything, I desperately longed to see her again.

I needed to exorcise this persistent ache in my throat, this overwhelming sorrow that consumed me whenever she entered my thoughts. But how could I possibly request such a meeting when I was the one who had abandoned her, failed her so completely, and bore responsibility for whatever pain she now carried? Would she believe I genuinely missed her, or would she assume I merely wanted to showcase my superiority over her current circumstances?

"If my father had ever discovered our relationship, he would have killed me." Those were her exact words, spoken with genuine terror in her voice.

Could I have been the reason for her life's ruin? Or perhaps other factors beyond my control conspired against her happiness? How desperately I wish she were here today. I needed to see her face, offer long overdue explanations, and stand beside her as she had once stood beside me. She had been my sanctuary during moments of exhaustion and despair. "You're weary? Then you need Lamees's gentle fingers and their miraculous healing touch."

"She remains unmarried." The thought immensely pleased me—how conveniently she should be unattached and potentially available. Surely, she wouldn't refuse a simple meeting with me? But did she retain that luminous beauty I remembered so vividly? God, how I missed her—and those golden, irrecoverable days.

What a contemptible, self-serving wretch I am. How dare I entertain such thoughts about her? After the devastating betrayal I inflicted, do I honestly expect her to welcome me with joy and throw herself into my arms once more? The notion is despicable, yet what power do I possess against these relentless desires? My body betrays me with its desperate longings.

Yet perhaps she still allows thoughts of me to occasionally drift through her consciousness. "She will never surrender her heart to another," Hanan had insisted, though she'd added ominously, "but she has undergone profound changes." Hanan had also mentioned barely recognizing her. What disturbing transformation could she have meant?

I forever envision her walking gracefully beneath the amber October sunlight across the courtyard of the Faculty of Arts. Her lustrous hair shines in the golden rays, paired with her enchanting smile that could stop my heart mid-beat.

Lamees had been radiant during those days—a freshman immersed in French literature while I pursued my senior studies in Ancient Languages. She was the unattainable dream of any student on campus: intoxicatingly beautiful, vibrantly alive, and playfully spirited. Every aspect of her being—her luminous smile, captivating glances, fluid movements, and distinctly feminine grace—made her utterly magnetic. I had never dared to assume I might capture her attention.

Then one extraordinary day, she approached me directly, her face illuminated by that signature smile, and spoke these words:

"Hello, I'm Lamees."

The introduction hit me like lightning—utterly unexpected and completely disarming. I stood frozen in astonishment as she continued with a charming blush and timidity:

"I notice you sometimes in the neighborhood. You're the one who came lately from Beirut, aren't you?"

Those simple words were all I needed to fall in love with her. I spent the entire night writing verses for her, even though I had no poet's gift—yet somehow the words flowed from my heart like rushing rivers while my longing descended in torrential downpours.

The next morning, I sought her out with unwavering determination and declared without any preliminary courtesies: "I believe I've fallen in love with you, Miss. I devoted the entire night to composing this poem in your honor."

She seemed stunned by my boldness, her silence speaking loudly as she processed the weight of my confession. I pressed the folded paper into her palm and left immediately, unable to endure the uncertainty of waiting for her response. Twenty-four hours later, she searched for me throughout the college grounds, ultimately delivering an answer that left me breathless:

"Forgive me, sir, but I fear you've arrived rather late to your revelation. Upon reading your words, I discovered I have loved you since immemorial."

Such was Lamees—direct, honest, and utterly captivating.

I proudly introduced her to my mother and sister, and soon she became a regular visitor to our home. She and Hanan formed an immediate and lasting friendship.

The memory of our first kiss remains eternally vivid in my mind. It happened on the narrow staircase connecting the first and second floors of our apartment building, exactly where our family apartment was. We had been leaving for the university during the afternoon siesta, when the world seemed to pause in drowsy quiet. The stairwell was deserted entirely, every neighboring door closed tight, and profound silence reigned—except for the thunderous cacophony in my head, where hormones surged like floodwaters and adrenaline turned my heartbeat into frantic percussion.

When she slipped her delicate hand into mine, I felt my entire being ignite. Some primal force compelled me to press her gently against the cool wall, and I claimed her lips with a kiss so passionate and consuming that it seemed to steal the very breath from her lungs. She was utterly innocent—a girl who had never experienced such intimate contact. As our lips finally parted, her eyes remained closed, and she whispered with breathless wonder: "Kiss me again."

I loved her with overwhelming intensity—I loved her body, her soul, her violent passion. I cherished her complete surrender, her awakening desire, and her uninhibited joy in our physical intimacy. She confessed to me with breathless sincerity: "I finally understand what I've been searching for in life. I know with absolute certainty that I belong to you forever."

With each passing day, my obsession with her only deepened.

Then, without warning, I awakened one morning to find myself delivering words that would shatter everything:

"We need to end this relationship."

"What? Why?" The shock struck her like a physical blow—she was sure I must be joking, unable to grasp such sudden cruelty.

"I'm completely serious. I believe we should separate. Please don't ask me to explain my reasons."

The truth was that her love had become a suffocating force, stealing the very air from my lungs. The strange thing is that I felt compelled to abandon her precisely because I loved her so desperately. I was drowning in the depths of her devotion until my own identity had completely dissolved. I could no longer distinguish where she ended and I began—I had lost myself entirely within her.

What did I truly want? I had no clear answer. Yet, somewhere in the distant recesses of my consciousness, an otherworldly melody beckoned—a mystical flute playing an entirely different song that demanded I close my eyes and surrender to its haunting call. I experienced an inexorable need to escape.

"What body could possibly be more beautiful than mine?" she pleaded desperately.

"There exists no other woman," I admitted with painful honesty.

"Then you're truly abandoning me?"

"I will return someday," I promised, even though I suspected the lie.

"How will I satisfy these desires you've awakened in me?"

And so, I left. I ran to America, leaving her to search desperately for explanations I didn't have. The humiliation of my cowardice burned inside me, yet I convinced myself that leaving was my only option.

"You won't recognize her anymore," Hanan had warned me with unmistakable sadness.

Guilt consumed me because I intimately understood how frustration and despair could ravage a person—how they wither natural beauty and extinguish the vital spark from once-luminous eyes, rendering them cold and lifeless. Had I truly been the architect of her life's destruction? These tormenting questions pursued me relentlessly. For a time, the vast distances of America granted me a reprieve from their accusations. But now they have returned with renewed vengeance, completely dominating my thoughts and refusing to grant me peace.

"A camera?" Hanan exclaimed with evident disappointment. "That's all there was? So, there's no treasure after all?"

Zeina laughed bitterly and addressed me with cutting sarcasm: "What a tragedy, uncle. The new car and villa with the swimming pool and my mother's grand delusions have evaporated."

"The mukhtar just telephoned to invite us all for dinner at his farm this evening," Hanan announced.

"OK, but now I'm considering visiting some old friends beforehand."

"Such as?"

"I thought I might call on Mustafa. I've completely lost touch with him, and I find myself missing his company."

The visit wasn't motivated purely by nostalgia—Mustafa had been integral to Lamees's and my social circle during university. He had been pursuing medical studies and hadn't yet graduated when I departed for America. Surely, he would possess current information about her circumstances. He came from an established, affluent family whose parents maintained a prestigious apartment in the distinguished Abu Rummaneh district.

Upon reaching his building, I discovered an impressive street-level medical clinic bearing his nameplate, though it appeared closed for the day. I ascended to the residential floors and pressed the doorbell.

When Mustafa answered, I greeted him with a warm smile, but he remained frozen in the doorway, visibly bewildered and taken aback by my unexpected appearance.

Eventually, he regained his composure enough to welcome me inside, although his demeanor fell considerably short of my expectations. Instead of the enthusiastic reunion I had anticipated, he appeared distinctly uncomfortable and strangely puzzled by my presence.

We settled into his elegant living room, exchanging perfunctory inquiries about each other's well-being. His nervousness became increasingly pronounced when his wife entered bearing a coffee service.

After introducing us, she joined our conversation with gracious hospitality. She was charming and articulate, contributing thoughtful observations to our discussion of various topics while listening attentively to our responses. Mustafa fell silent whenever she spoke, seeming content to let her dominate the conversation entirely.

After some time passed, I turned to Mustafa and asked a question that would shatter the evening's pleasant veneer: "How is Lamees these days? Have you had any recent contact with her?"

The effect was instantaneous and devastating. Mustafa and his wife lapsed into stunned silence, while perspiration formed visibly on his forehead. His wife's previously warm expression transformed into something far colder, her gaze fixing upon her husband with unmistakable fury as he refused to lift his eyes from the floor. I had never anticipated that my innocent inquiry would unleash such a reaction.

"I know nothing about her," he stammered, attempting unsuccessfully to keep calm.

"I haven't heard anything about her in years." His wife regarded him with a look of profound suspicion.

"My sister Hanan mentioned that she's teaching at the university now. Surely, you've encountered some news about her?"

"No, absolutely not," he insisted with barely controlled agitation. "As I've already stated, I know nothing about her circumstances." His tone carried such suppressed rage that I immediately recognized I had accidentally touched on a deeply sensitive and problematic subject.

His wife's friendly demeanor completely vanished, replaced by an arctic chill that filled the room. The oppressive silence that followed was so uncomfortable that I tried to change the subject of our conversation toward the professional achievements of Arab physicians in America. However, my efforts proved useless—she sustained her stony silence until finally I requested permission to withdraw from our gathering entirely.

She offered me a gracious farewell at the threshold, expressing hopes for a pleasant stay, while Mustafa escorted me toward the stairwell. There, he regarded me with profound gravity before speaking in hushed tones, having first confirmed his wife had withdrawn beyond earshot: "Listen carefully, Mamdouh. We have been friends—genuine friends—and that bond endures still. If you value my counsel, you would do well to forget her entirely and stay away from her."

He afforded me no opportunity to seek clarification or inquire what dark knowledge lay behind his warning. He had no intention of elaborating further. He retreated and sealed the door behind him abruptly, abandoning me to my confusion and astonishment.

That evening, we gathered at the mukhtar's countryside estate, where our host appeared notably spirited and convivial. Several of his children were present, creating a lively family atmosphere, yet Lamees remained absent.

"Where might Lamees be?" Hanan inquired with characteristic directness.

The question seemed to strike an uncomfortable nerve. I observed how everyone, instinctively, averted their gazes, each seemingly reluctant to provide an answer. Eventually, the mukhtar himself broke the awkward silence:

"I believe she has traveled to Homs for academic obligations—some lecture engagement that will prevent her from returning until next week at the earliest. Her professional commitments consume virtually all her time these days," the mukhtar's wife added hastily, attempting to provide additional justification. "Frankly, she rarely visits us anymore."

I was truly disappointed. I really longed to see her again and was quite curious about the changes she had supposedly undergone.

Despite this setback, the evening turned out to be thoroughly enjoyable. We shared plenty of laughter, engaged in a variety of conversations, and—most importantly—the mukhtar and I drank substantial amounts of alcohol. His wife made several attempts to moderate his drinking, citing concerns for his health, but he used my presence as perfect justification for celebration, encouraging even more indulgent consumption.

I found myself matching his pace drink for drink until my vision began to blur alarmingly. By the time we prepared to leave the farm, I had reached such a level of intoxication that maintaining my balance required conscious effort. The journey back to my apartment remains a complete mystery—I have no recollection of how I navigated the stairs or managed to find my bed. I, still fully clothed, collapsed into unconsciousness the moment my head touched the pillow.

Chapter Five

I once asked a colleague a question during my time in Los Angeles. We were seated outside, where a cat lay basking in a patch of sunlight, its unblinking gaze fixed on me with that peculiar, malicious intensity that seemed to penetrate right to one's soul.

"What do you suppose occupies a cat's thoughts?" I asked. "Do they harbor dreams, ambitions? Is it conceivable that their minds remain perpetually blank—that they think of nothing whatsoever during those long hours when they sit and stare?"

"Hardly," he replied with conviction. "They contemplate food constantly. And when they dream, they dream exclusively of sex."

I thought profoundly about his words, turning them over in my mind until I reached an unsettling realization: I am, in essence, a cat masquerading as a human being, for these two preoccupations—food and sex—consume the majority of my thoughts and fill every corner of my sleeping mind.

The apartment was enveloped in darkness and silence, interrupted only by the occasional murmur of passing cars on the street below, their headlights sweeping across the ceiling in fleeting arcs of light.

I had surrendered to deep sleep and found myself walking along a desolate beach, empty of people. The setting felt hauntingly familiar—I must have wandered this same beach in previous dreams.

A cool breeze caressed my skin while an overcast sky stretched endlessly above, its leaden expanse mirrored in the dark, restless waters below. The season appeared to be autumn, for I felt a penetrating chill. Someone must have suddenly stripped away my blanket, exposing me to the cold breeze.

A solitary figure occupied the beach—a young woman sitting on the sand, her gaze fixed contemplatively on the turbulent sea. I recognized her immediately. She's the one from my earlier dreams. Her delicate, silky dress fell gracefully along the curve of her legs, its border dancing in the gentle wind like a whispered invitation.

I approached with careful steps, eager not to startle her into flight as had happened in our previous encounters. This time, however, she turned to me with a shy, almost radiant smile. Her familiar features were partly obscured by loose strands of hair that the breeze had swept across her face like dark ribbons. She shifted her position slightly—a gesture so subtle yet unmistakable in its invitation that I understood I was meant to join her on the sand.

I settled into what I considered a respectful distance, yet I found my gaze irresistibly drawn to the elegant curve of her legs. She seemed completely unaffected by my admiring look. Indeed, she appeared almost pleased by the attention, which only intensified the current of desire coursing through my veins and made my heart pound against my ribs.

"Do you come here often?" I ventured, my voice barely audible above the whisper of wind and wave.

"Yes," she replied, the single word carrying the weight of countless unspoken secrets.

"Does my presence disturb you? I could sit elsewhere if you'd prefer."

"Not at all." Her voice held that same bashful quality that had first captivated me. "This beach belongs to everyone, after all. If anything, I'm grateful for your company."

Unbidden images flooded my mind—tender and urgent visions that ignited my blood. She reached for my hand and placed my palm against the warmth of her cheek.

"Your hand is cold," she observed. Then she pressed my fingers between her palms, breathing warm life into them before drawing them down to rest between her thighs. "Let me warm you."

Her body's heat flowed through my flesh like fire—more than just warmth; it awakened something ancient and primal within me, sending flames racing through every vein and artery. I felt paralyzed between desire and uncertainty. Should I lean forward and claim her lips? The urge swept through me like a tide, yet caution held me back. Could such beauty, such grace, truly be offering herself so freely? Perhaps her gestures came from innocence rather than invitation.

"You're trembling," she whispered, her voice like silk drawn across bare skin. "Come closer. Let me warm you."

Her arms enveloped me, drawing me into the soft warmth of her body until my face rested against her breast. Her heated breath scorched my throat as I remained still, content to exist in this perfect suspension of time, breathing the secret air between her breasts, drowning in that intoxicating fragrance that seemed both foreign and achingly familiar.

"Still shivering," she murmured, her fingers threading through my hair with endless tenderness.

I dared not make the slightest movement that she might misconstrue as presumptuous, still uncertain whether I was misreading signals born of mere kindness. Yet opportunity beckoned, and I knew

I must either seize it or watch it dissolve like morning mist. Tentatively, I let my fingers trace the length of her legs, marveling at the silk of her skin beneath my touch. She remained perfectly still, offering neither encouragement nor resistance. Then, with deliberate slowness, she began moving her hand downward along my body, movements both hesitant and unmistakably purposeful. Any doubt about her intentions evaporated like dew before the rising sun. I felt a profound relief wash over me—she would complete what she had begun.

My breathing became shallow and heavy as I desperately waited for her fingers to reach their destination. Somewhere in the distance, a car passed down the street, its headlights briefly turning the room ceiling above us into a canvas of shifting shadows.

She leaned in close, her lips brushing my ear as she whispered, "How does this feel? Are you comfortable with what I'm doing?"

"I pray I never wake from this dream, I confessed, I'm terrified of awakening, stealing you away from me. You will disappear."

"I will never disappear, she promised, I am here, beside you, as real as your heartbeat. Do you want me? Then release me and free me."

"What do you mean? I don't understand—"

I found myself suspended in that liminal space between dreaming and waking, and between sobriety and intoxication, with my entire being focused on the impending moment of ecstasy. I remained completely motionless, fearing that even the slightest movement could shatter this delicate reality and make her disappear.

But the perfume that enveloped her was more real than any dream, her warm breath against my neck more tangible than imagination could conjure, and the hand that now held me with such intimate authority was undeniably real.

"Am I truly dreaming?" I whispered into the darkness.

I opened my eyes to find myself enveloped in absolute night.

"Have I awakened, or am I still asleep?"

Only the eternal conversation between wave and shore reached my ears, punctuated by her urgent voice, almost commanding: "It doesn't matter now. Surrender. Don't be afraid."

Terror and bewilderment crashed over me in equal measure as I turned toward the sound of the sea. The waves maintained their ancient rhythm, advancing and retreating in endless cycles, and there was indeed a woman—flesh and blood and startling reality—whose body encircled mine, whose grip below had intensified to the very edge of pain. I struggled to move and free myself from her embrace, but I found myself utterly powerless against her strength.

"You are neither dream nor reality," I managed to say. "What are you?"

"I am your beloved," she breathed against my lips. "You don't have to be afraid."

Her mouth descended upon mine with sudden hunger, our breaths merging into a shared atmosphere. I felt her lips part mine and the warm invasion of her tongue claiming the depths of my mouth. All rational thought dissolved beneath the twin floods of lust and longing, and I surrendered to stillness, feeling her fingers slip beneath the barriers of clothing while my hands explored the territory of her body. Her breathing transformed into something urgent and primal as she began the ritual of undressing me, while I could barely raise enough strength to assist her efforts.

The symphony of waves crashing against the stone filled the air around us, their rhythm weaving together with her sighs and the soft sounds of pleasure that slipped from her lips. I could no longer distinguish between closed and open eyes, between the familiar geography of my bed and the vastness of this dream-like beach. Yet, her nakedness was undeniable, her body a warm weight enveloping me completely, and when she suddenly shook violently as if touched by lightning, I knew this was no mere figment of my sleeping consciousness.

Her teeth found the tender junction of my neck and shoulder, and she cried out in a voice raw with ecstasy, her breath coming in short gasps against my chest while her perfumed hair fell like a curtain across my face. Then her nails traced burning lines down my back, drawing from me a sharp cry of mingled pain and pleasure.

At that moment, as if summoned by some cosmic sense of timing, a small group materialized from the darkness—a man walking with his wife and a young girl whose beauty seemed to glow in the dim light. The girl's gaze found us immediately, her curiosity bare and unashamed, prompting me to whisper with desperate urgency:

"Dear God, people are watching us! Are we making love in full view of the world? Are you insane?"

I held my breath and pulled her tight against me, attempting to shield our nakedness from these unwelcome witnesses to our passion.

"Release me," she commanded, her voice suddenly strange and distant. "Free me and let me go."

The man continued his leisurely pace, seemingly oblivious to our presence. Still, his companions turned back repeatedly, their faces illuminated by expressions I couldn't quite decipher—amusement, perhaps, or knowing recognition.

"Don't you know who that is?" the woman said to her husband, her voice clear in the night air." He's the owner of the box."

I opened my eyes to find daylight streaming through familiar windows, harsh and unforgiving in its clarity. I was lying in my bed. My consciousness fractured into a thousand glittering pieces while confusion settled over my thoughts like fog. For long moments, I remained motionless, lacking the strength to lift even my face from the pillow. When I finally attempted to gather the scattered fragments of memory, everything remained maddeningly elusive, like trying to hold water in cupped hands.

Yet when I drew the pillow closer to my face, I caught the unmistakable trace of perfume—foreign and familiar all at once.

I forced myself upright and surveyed my surroundings with growing alarm. I was utterly alone, but the bed told a different story entirely. Sheets twisted all around, blankets flung to distant corners, my clothes scattered across the floor like the debris of some private catastrophe. And I was naked, my skin carrying the unmistakable musk of intimate encounter.

Rising on unsteady legs, I stood in the center of the room, terrified. Every detail of the night's events returned with crystalline clarity, yet the physical evidence of another's presence remained stubbornly absent. For nearly an hour, I searched every corner and shadow, desperate for concrete proof that I had not lost my mind entirely, but found nothing. Nothing at all.

The sound of waves continued their phantom crash inside my skull, accompanied by the memory of watching eyes and that woman's voice.

When I finally went to the bathroom, my reflection in the mirror revealed a story my rational mind refused to accept. Crimson lines traced paths across my torso where fingernails had marked their passage, while the evidence of teeth decorated my shoulders and throat.

I rushed to examine the outer door, finding it secured from within, its lock bearing no signs of tampering or forced entry. The apartment had been sealed tight as a tomb, yet somehow...

I collapsed onto the bed and squeezed my eyes shut, desperately trying to recapture even a fragment of that impossible dream. But the gateway had closed, leaving me stranded in a reality that felt infinitely more surreal than any fantasy my sleeping mind might have conjured.

Eventually, I returned to my sister's house, my equilibrium shattered and my thoughts lost in doubt and wonder. Nothing within me felt solid or dependable anymore. I stretched out on the sofa and closed my eyes, exhaustion and hunger battling for dominance in my drained body.

From somewhere far away, I heard Zeina's voice inviting me to join them for a meal, but sleep overtook me first—a deep, dreamless sleep that lasted until the sun had risen again. I woke up the next morning in a world that no longer made perfect sense.

Chapter Six

They say that the entire universe was a tiny dot of enormous energy, the size of a pinhead, in an eternal void since the beginning of time.

Then suddenly, for some unknown reason or on a whim, this energy exploded. Its fragments shot into the corners of space at unimaginable speeds, spread out, filled the void, and formed this wonderful and mysterious universe.

I always ask myself, "Can we go back to that point?"

My brother-in-law had already left by the time I woke up. I took a hot bath that rejuvenated me.

"You slept all day yesterday, you must have been very tired" said Zeina.

We had breakfast and then sat down to discuss Abu Jassim and what happened to him. Everyone shared their opinions and made various comments, but I felt a strange sensation as if I were floating in space.

The doorbell rang, Zeina looked at her mom, and they both smiled.

"Surprise." said Hanan

She stood up, opened the door, and returned with a smile.

"There's a guest in the living room that I want you to meet."

We stepped into the parlor, and it truly was a surprise.

There was a beautiful woman with soft, short hair that accentuated her long neck and a few strands that covered half of her face. She sat cross-legged, wearing a loose dress that draped freely just above her knees, leaving her legs exposed. She looked at me with a familiar smile. Then, she got up from her seat and extended her hand.

"Welcome back, Dr. Mamdouh."

I extended my hand as I stared at her, mesmerized by her beauty. She smiled and mumbled a few words. I didn't know what to say to her because she laughed that familiar and endearing laugh. I couldn't believe my eyes. Her beauty hadn't faded, and the light in her eyes hadn't gone out; on the contrary, she radiated vitality and femininity. My sister didn't lie when she said, "You won't recognize her," but I was foolish, and my imagination went in the opposite direction. That's how narcissism is, and that's how I am. I always think I'm the center of the universe, that girls adore the ground I walk on, and that if I abandon one of them, she'll die of heartbreak. As if there's no other man in the world. How arrogant I am. How foolish. Here she is: "Lamees," shining with joy, femininity, and vitality. She exceeded all my expectations.

"Why are you staring at me like that?"

"I'm searching for Lamees."

She laughed and said, "Did you find her?

"No."

"Then what did you find?"

"I don't know. But the little girl has gone."

"You mean you used to see me as a child?"

"No, but now I see what childish I was."

"Anyway, do you like what you found?"

"I am Surprised and delighted."

"Were you expecting this visit?"

"Not at all. Your father said you were in Homs."

Yes, I was. I came right away when your sister called and told me you were back.

Hanan smiled slyly and said, "I went through a lot of trouble to get her number."

"You didn't answer, did you like or dislike the surprise?"

I'm very pleased; I was looking forward to meeting you.

She didn't take her eyes off me, and her smile didn't fade the whole time.

"You've changed so much. That sparkle in your eyes, I almost didn't recognize you. I wasn't expecting that."

"What did you expect? Did you expect to see shrapnels?" she said in a quiet, sarcastic voice.

"I don't know what to say, and I don't know what made me think you were unhappy."

"Maybe that's what your subconscious wants to find."

"No, not at all, even in my deepest depths, I wish you happiness; you can say it was my stupidity that made me misjudge you. I admit you have exceeded all my expectations, and I am happy about it—happy to see you still as beautiful and bright as I knew you to be."

She didn't react. I continued in a low voice, "You can't imagine how much I blame myself for what I did to you and to me. I will never be able to justify what I did."

Lamees was sitting quietly, listening, her eyes checking my facial expressions and scrutinizing the way I spoke. It wasn't like her; she was too shy to stare into my eyes. Her calmness made me feel how powerful she is and how vulnerable I am.

"There was no other girl. You know that."

"Yes, I know that."

I gazed into her eyes and said:

"Will you forgive me?"

She remained silent, looking at me quietly, and then she said with a smile:

"Don't make a big deal out of it, can't you see that I'm fine?"

"But I'm not. I still feel guilty and ashamed. Your calmness and smile hurt me more and more. I wish you would curse me or even hit me."

I took her hand and put it on my cheek:

"I wish you would slap me, or maybe it's better if you drive your car over my body, or push me from the top of the mountain into a deep abyss, and then roll a big boulder over me, maybe I would feel better."

Lamees laughed and said, "Now I understand why I once loved you. You are strong and can make a comedy out of tragedy."

I am now a pile of despair and frustration. I wish you would yell at me. I can't hurt you; I don't want to. I understand what happened. It was going to happen one day or another. This is the nature of things.

"How much your words hurt me."

"Look, Mamdouh, I got over it a long time ago. Don't make a big deal out of it; I'm not a child, and I've never been weak. I'm not the kind of person who falls apart easily. It's just that you surprised me, that's all. I was a bit dazed; I almost lost my confidence at first when I was looking for answers within myself."

"And did you find them?"

It took a few failed relationships with men to realize that the problem was you, not me.

"Was Dr. Mustafa one of them?"

Lamees burst out laughing. She looked at me with surprised eyes.

"Mustafa? What do you know about my relationship with him?"

I visited him yesterday. I asked him about you in front of his wife. The question caused quite a stir. He whispered to me later to stay away from you. What did you do to him?

"Poor Mustafa, he's so good. But he's afraid to face himself and doesn't know what he wants."

"And you, do you know what you want?"

Yes, I know exactly what I want, and I knew exactly what he wanted.

"What about me? What do I want?"

Lamees smiled: "You are something else."

"Your words scare me. Tell me honestly, have you come to take revenge on me?"

She laughed and said, "Did you think so?" I didn't answer but kept looking into her eyes, she looked at me with serious eyes and repeated again:

"Did you think that? No, not at all, don't think for a moment that I have anything against you."

She came closer to me and put her palms on my face, and planted a kiss on my lips as she whispered

"I could never hate you. You were the best thing that ever happened to me, and you still are. You were the best friend and the best lover. I've never loved a man like you."

"You know, I never stopped loving you." I realize it now; I thought I'd forgotten you, but you came back and blew it all up.

I was so excited by the warmth of her breath, the scent of her perfume, and the delicacy of her whisper that I closed my eyes and heard the roar of the waves on the beach. Yesterday's dream was still fresh in my mind. I glimpsed the ghost of a tear in her eyes, and I let my hand rest in her lap while my other hand reached out to caress her leg.

"Don't mistake my coming to see you," she said as she took my hand off her leg and gently pushed me away.

"So you're still mad at me."

"Never, you are closer to me than my heart. I've never loved anyone as much as I've loved you, and I don't think I ever will."

I tried to reach out to her again, but she pushed me away again and stood up, apologizing for pushing me away:

"I don't want you to be angry with me or hate me."

"So what do you want from me?"

"Nothing."

"Then why did you come?"

"Don't I have the right to love you and miss you?"

Lamees left after she set me on fire and left me to burn. Her visit remained a mystery to me, leaving me frustrated and hopeless.

After she left, I thought about every word she said. I analyzed it and tried to get to the bottom of it. But all that did not lead to a result, except that it introduced doubt into my mind about the woman in the dream. Could it be Lamees?

I asked my sister: "Who has the key to my apartment?"

"No one. Why do you ask that question? Is something missing?

"No, but do you remember the night we went to the mukhtar's farm and you drove me back home?"

"Yes, you were almost unconscious."

I laughed and asked who drove me to the apartment.

"My husband and I."

"I wonder if you locked the door when you left?"

"Of course we did. Did something happen? Was anything stolen? Why are you asking all these questions?" I ignored her question. How could I tell her about the dream that night? Or was it not a dream?

"Did Lamees find out that I returned from traveling that night?"

"I don't think so, because I informed her of your arrival the next day."

"Where was she then?"

"You know she was in Homs."

"How do we know for sure? Couldn't she have been in Damascus?"

My sister thought for a while and admitted she could have been in Damascus. "But does it matter?

Why are you asking all these questions? Did something happen that night?"

"I just wonder why she didn't come to the soiree if she was in Damascus?"

My sister laughed: "Maybe because she wasn't in Damascus, but in Homs."

Chapter Seven

In my dreams, I experience the sweetest fantasies. For moments, my most challenging desires come true, alongside my worst nightmares. But ultimately, they remain just dreams and nightmares. Sometimes, I wake up feeling disappointed because I arose before fulfilling a desire I was pursuing, and other times, I breathe a sigh of relief, thankful that what I was experiencing was merely a nightmare that vanished with the dream.

What if I could connect the dream to reality? What if the dream continued and became reality, or reality turned into a dream? What if the figures from my dreams stepped out to stand in front of me in reality?

The next morning, I woke up to Al Mukhtar's phone call. He was nervous.

"Abu Anwar called me, he wants us in his office right away, so get ready, I'll pick you up right now."

"I hope it's for something good."

"It seems to have something to do with the camera."

"What about it?"

"I don't know, but he's very upset. I'm coming, I won't be long."

I was a little worried. But I was relieved that Al Mukhtar would be with me.

Abu Anwar's office was on the second floor of the Bab Musalla police station, which was very crowded. I walked behind the mukhtar as he was pushing people in front of him, and climbed the stairs with the energy of a young man, or so he tried to show me. We reached the office. The door was closed.

"Strange, said the Mukhtar, he had never closed his office door before."

We knocked and entered. The room was a mess. It was filled with shelves, papers, files, and folders. Abu Anwar sat behind his desk with a pale face, lost in thought, staring at the camera on the desk. He looked at us without smiling.

The camera has been checked. There's nothing unusual about it. It's old, very old; it can't take more than one picture at a time.

He fell silent.

I said in a hesitant voice, "Can I take it back then?"

He gave me an angry look and said, "Take it."

Hesitantly, I took it off the desk, slowly and with caution, his eyes never leaving it. The Mukhtar asked him, "Was there a picture in it?"

"Yes, there was a picture in it. Then he looked at me angrily and said:

"Damn you, your father, the camera and the photo."

I looked at the Mukhtar, and he looked back at me puzzled. The Mukhtar asked, "Why do you say that, Abu Anwar? Was there something wrong in the photo?"

"I tried to tear it up, he said, but I couldn't. Even the technicians tried to burn it, but they failed. Can you imagine?"

"Why do you want to burn and destroy it?" I asked him curiously.

"Because it's haunted."

"What?"

"Yes, it's haunted by jennies and goblins."

I tried to stifle my laughter, but it didn't work. Abu Anwar looked at me angrily:

"You think I'm dumb, don't you? Here, take a look."

He picked up an envelope from the desk, opened it, took out a picture, and handed it to me.

It was strange.

In the photo, Abu Jassim and Abu Anwar stood exactly where they were when the picture was taken at Abu Jassim's house. In the background, a woman's face appeared, her hair flying wildly across the image, stretching her arms into the air as if she were floating in space. The woman was incredibly beautiful and almost naked, but her gaze was so unusual that I shuddered when I looked into her eyes.

"Who is this woman?" asked the Mukhtar.

"That's what I want to know from Mr. Mamdouh."

"I don't know this woman at all. I've never seen her face. How did she come into the picture?"

The technicians say that she was already in the film when the picture of me with Abu Jassim appeared above it, meaning that they are two pictures superimposed on one another.

"So what's the issue? Why are you upset? It's just a picture," I said, trying to calm him down.

"Don't you see how she looks at me? How she stares at me? Her eyes never leave my mind; my body has been shaking ever since I saw them. I see them everywhere I turn. Her gaze gnaws at my bones and burns my nerves. I can't think anymore; I can't work, I can't work. I want to get rid of her image in my mind, but I can't."

"You're exaggerating, it's true that her gaze is strange. But she is beautiful. Can't you see that?" said the Mukhtar, looking at the photo and laughing. "You made me leave my office and come in a hurry for a photo of a woman."

He took a pair of scissors from his drawer and tried to cut the picture, but the scissors couldn't cut it.

"Isn't that strange?"

The phone rang. Abu Anwar answered it, started talking, then quickly hung up and said: "It's Abu Jassim's wife, something is wrong with him, she wants us to come quickly. Let's go."

He put the photo back in the drawer. At the office door, before leaving the room, Abu Anwar asked us: "Does Abu Jassim know you are here?"

"No," replied the Mukhtar

"Then how did his wife know you were here?"

She said, "Come, you, the mukhtar, and Mr. Mamdouh, who are in your office."

When we arrived, Abu Jassim's wife welcomed us, but she was confused:

Thank God you came. I don't know what to do or how to deal with Abu Jassim. The loss of his sight will drive him crazy, or he may have already lost his mind. As you can see, he is acting like a madman or a drunkard, moving in all directions, stumbling, falling, and then getting back up again.

"What's wrong with him?" I asked. "What happened?"

Abu Jassim heard me and turned to me in despair and frustration:

"Tell me, Mr. Mamdouh, weren't you wearing a blue striped shirt yesterday?"

"yes," I replied

"That's exactly what I'm saying, and it's almost driving me crazy. I saw you, I saw your shirt, and you were holding the camera, believe me. It was just for one moment. And that's when the flash went off."

"Okay, calm down. Maybe it was so bright that it nearly blinded us all."

"What's even more amazing is that today, since this morning, I've been seeing different faces and different scenes, as if I'm watching a TV screen. The

Mukhtar looked at me, then at his silent wife, and shook his head in regret. He said, "May Allah help you."

"I am not crazy, Mukhtar, I saw Abu Anwar with my own eyes, and I saw you and Mr. Mamdouh, I mean I saw your picture in my mind, you were in Abu Anwar's office. Believe me, you were looking at me and staring at me, you were in his office. Sometimes, I saw the fan on the ceiling of his office, and there were faces of people staring at me, including people who work in Abu Anwar's office. It would last a few minutes, and then it would get dark again as if I were watching TV. I'm going crazy. What is happening to me?"

"Well, are you still seeing these things at this moment?" I asked him.

"No, now it's all gone, there's nothing, just total darkness, the darkness of the blind."

"Then calm down, you must be exhausted, it's the only explanation. Take a tranquilizer and get some rest. Have you seen a doctor?"

"Believe me, I'm not sick. Shall I describe your clothes? Well, Mukhtar wears trousers and a khaki shirt. Mr. Mamdouh is wearing a white shirt with brown stripes. Am I wrong?"

He was right. It surprised me and all of us. We couldn't explain what was going on.

"It's all strange," said the mukhtar. "First, the box, then the camera, then the picture, and now this?"

"'What picture?'" said Abu Jassim.

"It's the photo of you and Abu Anwar, Said the Mukhtar—the one that Mr. Mamdouh took of you. A woman appeared with you in the photo."

Umm Jassim screamed." It's the curse of the box. It all started when we dug in the garden and the box appeared. It's cursed, and this woman you say appeared in the photo must be a fairy or a jinni.

"What do you think, Abu Anwar?" asked the Mukhtar. But Abu Anwar was drowsy, deep in thought, and not commenting on anything. I whispered in the Mukhtar's ear: "Can I leave now?"

"Please don't leave," Abu Jassim said.

"What do you want from me?"

"I want to apologize to you and ask your forgiveness. I want to come to a compromise with you. I think what is happening is a sign of anger; someone wants revenge on me. Listen, Mr. Mamdouh, I want to compensate you for my illegal presence in the house for the past few years."

"You won't pay him anything," Abu Anwar barked.

"Abu Anwar, speak for yourself, I can't stand it anymore, I'm almost suffocating. Ever since I started seeing those images, I feel like I'm in a grave, I can't stand the darkness, I can't breathe anymore, I can't breathe."

"Are you going crazy?" Abu Anwar said nervously, "Isn't what I've been through today enough? And now you are seeing things, hallucinating, and acting crazy. Leave me alone and go to hell."

Abu Anwar walked out without a word, while Abu Jassim's voice followed him:

"Why don't you believe me? I see things I don't understand. But I did see you and some of the people in the office."

"This is a surprise I didn't expect. I said to Abu Jassim: In any case, I don't want any money from you, Abu Jassim, I just want the house back, it's a precious memory of my father"

After everyone calmed down, I asked for permission to leave, and Abu Jassim said in a decisive voice, "I still stand by my word on the issue of the house, and tomorrow we will continue our conversation. Tomorrow, I will inform you of my decision."

I left and went to my sister's house. I showed her the camera. She didn't recognize it. When I told her about the photo and what happened with Abu Anwar and Abu Jassim, she became scared.

I didn't know that the mystery would become even more mysterious and that tomorrow would bring a big surprise.

The next morning, I went to Abu Jassim's house. He was waiting for me, looking nervous. His wife served me tea, and we sat on the porch overlooking the garden. He drank his tea silently and anxiously. Suddenly, he said, "He's been staring at me since this morning?"

"Who?"

Abu Anwar. I've been seeing him staring at me since this morning. His face is covered with fear. I could swear his hair is whiter than it was yesterday.

"Do you see him at this moment?"

"Yes. He's in his office. Do you want me to describe it? I see the ceiling light and the fan. Sometimes I see the wall behind his desk."

"Do you see me in front of you now?"

"No, I don't. You don't believe me?"

"I'm trying to believe you, but I don't understand what you're going through. I don't understand how you can see him in his office and not see me in front of you?"

Suddenly, he jumped to his feet and started screaming.

"Save Abu Anwar, someone save him!" I rushed to calm him down and asked his wife to call the mukhtar. Abu Jassim continued to panic, saying, "Something happened to Abu Anwar."

"What happened to him?"

"I don't know, but something scared him and made his eyes widen in terror."

Abu Jassim remained agitated, babbling Abu Anwar's name until the mukhtar came with the doctor. The doctor gave him a tranquilizer pill and told him to rest, but he didn't rest until the mukhtar called Abu Anwar's office, and there was the surprise:

Abu Anwar had a sudden heart attack and was taken to the hospital.

Abu Jassim jumped out of his chair: "Didn't I tell you? I saw him, I saw the signs of terror on his face."

"I believe you, I said, as strange as it sounds, because everything you say turns out to be true. Tell me, what do you see now?"

"I see the fan in the ceiling of his office."

"What do you say," I asked the mukhtar standing in confusion, "what if we go to Abu Anwar's office? Take us there, let's see what's with the ceiling. This is a serious matter that needs to be followed up."

We went to Abu Anwar's office. Abu Hamza, the mukhtar, known to everyone in the police station, got us into Abu Anwar's office.

The desk was covered with numerous papers and documents, and atop them all was the photo. I picked it up and started to scrutinize it.

"Do you see anything unusual in it, Abu Hamza?"

"Other than the woman with the charming eyes, I don't see anything worth mentioning."

The Mukhtar's phone rang, and Abu Jassim was shouting on the other end:

"I can see you both, you and Mr. Mamdouh."

"Describe what you see?" I asked him. The photo was in my hands, and he described more details in the office as I moved around the room.

Suddenly, the mukhtar shouted with excitement: "I found it, now I know, now I figure it out. It's the picture."

"What about it?"

He said excitedly:

"Don't you see? He is seeing through the picture". He pointed the picture towards the wall and asked Abu Jassim on the other side: "What do you see now?" He described the contents of the wall, including cabinets, shelves, and pictures.

The most amazing thing was that he could only see through his own eyes. If Mukhtar covered the picture with his hands, then Abu Jassim couldn't see anything. We put the photo back in its envelope and set off toward Abu Jassim's house. When we arrived, Abu Jassim greeted us eagerly: "What did you find? Tell me, do you know what's going on?"

The mukhtar took the picture out of its envelope, placed it in front of Abu Jassim's eyes, and asked him, "What do you see?" He said in amazement, "I see myself as if I'm looking at myself in the mirror. That's me."

Then he turned it towards us and said, "Now I see you." He held the picture in his hands and eagerly pointed it around, exclaiming, "I can see, I see everything, I see you, Umm Jassim, I see all of you."

"It's a miracle," said the Mukhtar.

"Or maybe a curse," Abu Jassim suddenly commented, "Look what happened to Abu Anwar? By the way, where is he now?" he asked.

"In the hospital," I said

"Listen, Mr. Mamdouh, I have made up my mind. I will leave you the house as soon as possible. I will pay you all the rent due from the past years, and then I will ask for your forgiveness. I hope this may be enough to prevent the curse of the box and the picture."

When I told Hanan about how things had evolved, she was scared

Maybe he's right. Do you think the camera is actually haunted, as they say?

I said confidently and with the firmness of one who wants to calm her down:

"No."

"Then how do you explain what's happening?" Zeina said, with fear showing all over her face.

"There must be a scientific answer to all of this. But I don't have it right now."

In fact, I didn't have answers to anything, and I was unable to explain any of the events that occurred during this week, including the woman in the dream, the box, the camera, the photo, and the strange phenomenon affecting Abu Jassim, as well as what happened to Abu Anwar. The mystery surrounded me on all sides and left me feeling unbalanced. The problem was that each riddle attracted another mystery.

In the evening, the mukhtar came to visit me at the apartment. I was glad to see him, not only because he was Lamees's father, but also because I had no friends to turn to. Lamees was inaccessible to me, Mustafa had a strange attitude towards me, and I didn't think he and his wife would feel comfortable with my visit. I was experiencing a stage of frustration along with feelings of loneliness and emptiness, so that whenever I lay on the bed, I hoped for a miracle that would bring me Lamees. I felt lonely and empty, and all I wanted at that moment was to talk to her, to hold her, to kiss her. Just the thought of her excited me. The change in her and the mystery surrounding her made her even more thrilling and lovable than before, increasing my fondness for her and my determination to win her back.

The Mukhtar could have been my friend as he had shared the strange events with me and was very friendly, but unfortunately, he was also Lamees' father. I could never tell him how I felt about her. He came to take me to visit Abu Anwar in the hospital. They had moved him out of the intensive care room, but he never emerged from the silence and stillness he was in. He was in a mental coma and a constant state of stupor.

The mukhtar's attempts to get his attention through conversation were unsuccessful. The lieutenant remained silent and isolated. While looking at him sadly, the Mukhtar said, "Isn't it strange what happened to him? I wonder what suddenly struck him and made him in this state?" Abu Jassim says that he was staring at the picture. What did he see in it that frightened him so much?

"I think He saw himself."

Don't be so harsh; there must have been something that frightened him. Something we didn't notice. We were glancing at it quickly and carelessly; we didn't scrutinize it closely. He must have seen something that caused him so much grief.

I laughed: "It's the way you talk like this that scares me."

We need to take another look at it. How about we head over to Abu Jassim's right now?

Abu Jassim lay on the couch on the balcony, cradling the picture. He handled it carefully, rotating it in every direction as if it were a lamp illuminating things in the dark. He pointed the picture toward us, as if he were shining a light on something. He greeted us:

"I can see you now. I got out of the house today, can you believe it? I was able to walk down the street with the help of the photo."

"That's good" I replied.

"But people were afraid, everyone who knew the photo's story said that a spirit was living in it."

I tried to calm him down: "Do you believe them?"

He said sadly, " I am scared, and my fear increases every time I think about what would happen if the picture is torn or lost? It controls my fate now, and I don't know how to deal with it and keep it safe."

"Calm down a little, this riddle must come to an end and will be solved", said the mukhtar.

"I couldn't sleep a wink."

"Mr. Mamdouh and I want to examine the photo"

"What are you looking for exactly?"

"Honestly, we don't know, but there must be something in it that causes what is happening to you and Abu Anwar. Have you examined it?"

"You know I can't. Every time I look at it, all I see is myself."

Mukhtar took the photo from him, placed it on the table in front of me, and sat beside me, examining it and muttering:

"There was nothing unusual; Abu Anwar, next to him, Abu Jassim in his chair. I'm sure the secret is in this woman; there's something unusual about her. Is it in her eyes? In her hair? In her hands? Then he fell silent and suddenly shouted: "Am I seeing right?" He put on his glasses.

"Even with my glasses, I can't believe what I'm seeing."

Then he handed me the glasses:

"Take my glasses and look at the watch in her hand. Do you see what I see? Does that make sense?"

I put on his glasses and looked at the picture, and asked him: "What did you see?"

"Look closely at her hand."

"There's a watch on her wrist."

"Look closely at the watch."

"It's a regular watch with a red heart-shaped background."

"There's something else."

"Oh my God, I yelled. You are right. It's unbelievable. "

Um Jassim screamed: What is it? What did you see? Let me see.

"Come and look."

I pointed my finger at the watch

"Check it." When Um Jassim saw the watch, she screamed in fear, turned away, and threw the picture on the ground.

"Abu Jassim said, "What's wrong with you? What did you see? Umm Jassim said in horror: "The watch hands are moving."

"What? Are the hands moving in the picture? "

"Yes, as if it's coming to life, this must be what frightened Abu Anwar," said Um Jassem.

"The hands are moving?" Abu Jassim said in horror, "It is indeed an enchanted picture. I'm scared."

"Why, what frightens you?"

"I'm thinking of what will happen to me. It is clear that this woman is targeting Abu Anwar and me because we are with her in the picture. Look what she did to Abu Anwar."

"Don't be pessimistic," I said. "She didn't harm you. On the contrary, if you're seeing now, it's thanks to her and through her, so she is of benefit to you."

"The problem is that I don't know her intentions and what she hides from me. That's what scares me."

Chapter Eight

We walked out of Abu Jassim's house, all of us stunned by what had occurred. The mukhtar was providing explanations one after another. Yet each explanation led to more questions and deeper mysteries.

I left the mukhtar and wandered alone through the streets at night, searching for old friends in familiar neighborhoods. There were a lot of questions in my mind. Yet one thing I knew for sure was that I was the subject of this mystery, and everything that was happening was meant for me.

After a futile search, I found myself calling Lamees. Her voice was bright when she answered:

"Hello, Mamdouh.'

"How are you, Lamees?"

"I'm fine. What about you? Are you okay?"

"I need to see you now."

"I don't think it's a good idea."

"It's very serious."

"You're worrying me, what's this serious issue?" she said, looking worried.

"I'm hungry,"

"Oh my God, you made my heart drop."

"Doesn't it matter to you that I'm hungry? Doesn't it matter to you that I, Mamdouh, am hungry and longing to meet you? Doesn't it satisfy your ego that I'm begging to see you?"

"You're still as arrogant as ever. Oh, how I long for your arrogance."

"I tell you that my dignity is shattered at your feet, and you say I'm arrogant?"

"I've already had my dinner. It's late now."

"Forget about food; I just want to see you."

"You look anxious, I've never seen you like this."

"There's so much going on that I don't understand, and I don't feel good about it. I need you. I need to talk to you."

"At this late hour?"

"Why not? Tell me honestly, is there a man with you now? Is there another man in your life?".

"You know very well that you're not just anyone to me, and that no man can keep me from you if I want you."

"Do you mean that?"

"I mean it."

"So, do you still love me?"

She was silent for a moment, then said: "Okay, give me an hour, then come to my house."

I soared with happiness; I was confident I could move her emotions and win her back because I was serious and honest with her. I was beginning to realize that my feelings for her were genuine, not just a tactic to get her back. She is Lamees, and I am Mamdouh, and what we shared was something strong that time cannot erase.

She provided me with the address; her home was an apartment in one of the towers in the Dummar high area, west of Damascus.

Exactly an hour later, I rang the doorbell. Her words, "No man can keep me from you," made my heart sing with joy. Lamees opened the door. As always, she looked elegant and beautiful. I glanced at her from head to toe. "You're becoming more elegant and sexy, do you know that?"

She smiled, and the scent of her perfume when she kissed me on the cheek nearly blew my mind. I hugged her; she didn't mind but gently pushed me away, took my hand, and led me into the living room. Her apartment was spacious; next to the main living room was a dining room surrounded by rooms on all sides. We sat on a couch in the living room. Her books and papers were scattered across the carpet. "Excuse me, I was working."

We sat next to each other, and everything about her was seductive: her dress, her exposed breasts, and her legs. She smiled and said, "You look tired and worn out."

"I've been through some strange events lately, your father must have told you that."

"I don't see him much, but you can tell me yourself."

I started talking, and she listened, but I could tell she wasn't interested and was faking it. I cut myself off abruptly and just looked at her silently; she felt distant, not like the person who used to tell me, "you need Lamees' fingers and palms"; that's what she would say to me in such situations. And she would end up in my lap before I could finish. That's how I knew her and what I needed right now.

"What is it? Why did you stop?"

I don't think you're interested in hearing my bullshit. I'm boring you; I can feel it... I feel like

I've lost you and won't get you back. It hurts. I know it's all my fault, and I don't blame you.

"I told you I'm over it now. You should be over it, too. Don't worry about me; I'm fine."

"How can I not worry when I still love you, but feel like you're still mad at me and treat me with contempt? I thought things were back to normal on the phone and was so happy. I told myself, here we are again, the good old days."

"But we've changed; I'm not the same Lamees you remember, and you're not the Mamdouh I once knew. We're two people who've grown. I think we've changed for the better. And I still love you more than ever."

She paused for a moment, then smiled, took my hand, and said, "Come with me."

She led me into the bedroom where a large bed occupied the center. She sat down beside me, her dress slipping off much of her body.

I grabbed her hand, kissed it, and continued smiling: "Now I need Lamees' fingers."

She smiled and said, "Ah, you still remember that?"

I reached out to hug her, but she gently pushed me away with a smile, quietly got up, closed the bedroom door, and turned off the lights.

It was dark. I heard her approach the bed and sit next to me. I touched her. She was naked. I hugged her and kissed her lips. A kiss full of lust and memories. She was soft and malleable in my hands, but she was silent, and I could only hear the sound of her successive breaths. She took off my clothes to let her fingers flow freely over my body and play with every part of it, up and down. Her lips greedily caressed my mouth and tongue. The room was pitch black, and I could smell her scent but could only see her ghost. She had taken complete control, leaving me to her whims. She finally let out a muffled scream and collapsed on my chest, panting with exhaustion. I stayed still for a moment, waiting for her breath to subside. Then I kissed her and let her lie next to me, relaxed. I felt happy and relieved about how things turned out. I closed my eyes to nap, but suddenly felt a movement beside the bed. I thought I saw someone sitting in the corner. Panicked, I turned on the room's light to confront a sight I had never imagined. Lamees sat on the sofa opposite the bed, fully clothed. In the bed was another woman, naked. She was bare. The surprise was so overwhelming that I didn't know what to say and did not react immediately. Lamees looked at me with a strange expression I couldn't understand, a ghost of a smile on her lips. My mind raced to analyze the situation, but I couldn't grasp anything. I felt angry, but this time it was something deeper than anger: fear and despair. The first thought that struck me, which quickly depressed me, was that Lamees had been lost to me forever. That thought unleashed all the sadness, fear, and anger within me. I finished getting dressed without uttering a word, avoiding eye contact with her. I sat on the edge of the bed with a lump in my throat.

"Believe me, it's better to leave her alone."

Those were Mustafa's words that I remembered in my labyrinth. I wonder if that's what he meant?

Lamees was still staring silently at the air while the woman in the bed lay there, looking at me and smiling.

"Is that a tear in your eye?" Her question surprised me. I didn't know what to reply.

"No, a cockroach suddenly entered my eye, crying out for help."

"That's what I love about you," she said, laughing

"What is that?"

"You're strong. I admit that. I wish I were like you."

"Why do you think I'm strong? Do you know that if you drive your car over me, or make a train hit me, or even if you throw me off a mountain and roll a big rock over me, it wouldn't hurt as much as it does now. God, how cruel and evil you are."

"Why are you so angry?" She approached me and sat down next to me, grabbed my hand and started running my hand over her lips, kissing her as she closed her eyes, then running it down her cheek, then her neck, and finally down to her breasts. I pulled my hand away violently and stood up to leave:

"How can you love me and do this to me? What do you want from me?"

Her eyes were full of tears. and like a child begging for forgiveness, she said:

"Please don't be angry. I can't allow myself to hurt you. You are my biggest dream and the best thing that ever happened to me."

"You are crazy. Now I understand why Mustafa warned me about you."

I said that and walked out of her apartment; I didn't wait for an explanation; I wasn't ready to understand anything then.

I wandered through empty streets and dark alleys, hiding from neon and car lights until I reached my apartment. The weight of the event pressed heavily on my chest; I was tired of thinking and utterly exhausted. Once inside, I didn't come out for an entire day. My phone rang constantly; all the incoming calls were from Lamees. I didn't answer them; I turned my phone off and fell into a coma-like sleep.

The ghost of Lamees haunted me day and night; she was engraved in my mind. I couldn't shake her from my thoughts, nor escape her presence in my dreams.

I heard Hanan's voice saying, "He has a high fever," and then I felt the sting of cold water on my forehead. I opened my eyes. Zeina was smiling anxiously as she placed cold water compresses on my forehead.

"You shouldn't have stayed alone in the apartment, and you shouldn't have turned off your phone. How do you feel now?"

I lifted my head and felt slightly dizzy.

"How could it be possible that you've been in the apartment alone for two days?" Hanan said, "If the mukhtar hadn't called to ask about you, we would have thought you were still with him. Why didn't you call us?"

"I must've been really tired."

"Is it all because of the photo and the camera? You have to forget all that or you'll hurt yourself."

Two days later, I'd recovered from the fever and reached out to the mukhtar, who was more than happy to take my call.

"Hey, how are you? What happened to you? Is it the curse of the photo, too?"

"No, no, it's just exhaustion and fatigue."

When he learned about my illness, he chose to visit me right away. The mukhtar appeared exhausted, looking weary and sleep-deprived.

"You don't look so good either, Abu Hamza. Are you feeling okay?"

"I'm tired of thinking about the past two days; the story of the camera and the photo has taken over my mind. It's not just an ordinary event. It's as if the picture is a living thing or a living being trapped inside it." He paused for a moment and then asked me:

"Do you believe in metaphysics?"

"supernatural? You mean jinn and goblins?"

"Yes"

"So, you think a fairy or jinni is behind this picture?"

"You don't think so?"

"I don't know, I'm not sure I can tell you anything about that," I said, laughing. "I've never met them in person, to be honest. I think there's a scientific explanation for everything, but I can see why people believe in them. I'm no better than they are, and I don't have an answer for their beliefs. What's your take on it?"

"I'm exhausted from thinking about it. I'm at a loss for any other explanation, and to be honest, I'm scared. I'd love to hear your thoughts."

"I aim to think scientifically."

"Me too, and I raised my kids that way, but even so, most of the time I'm comfortable attributing my mistakes to bad luck or envy."

"That's comforting too, but it's not the answer; there's always a logical and convincing scientific answer."

"Sometimes I prefer to be convinced in any way, even without logic. Most of the answers we receive lack logic, yet we remain convinced. That woman's gaze still gives me goosebumps."

"Don't you think the look in her eyes might be due to fear? I mean, she might be scared herself and not trying to intimidate us."

"What do you mean?"

"I think jinn, if they exist, might be poor creatures, and they are likely more afraid of us than we are of them."

"Honestly, don't you ever think jinn might be behind what's going on?"

"I agree it's strange and unnatural, but we shouldn't jump to conclusions until we have all the facts."

"What facts? "

"First, we need to know where the camera came from, and then who is the woman in the photo?"

"Do you realize this is the second completely illogical thing that's happened to me since the incident with Lamees?"

"Lamees?"

"Yes, Lamees, my daughter. Something strange happened to Lamees when she was a child, and I witnessed it."

"You've piqued my curiosity."

"I'll tell you what happened to her. I've shared this story many times, but I stopped long ago because no one believes me—not even Lamees herself."

"What happened to her?"

"One day, Lamees returned from school in tears. She was eleven years old. Her teacher had punished her for not memorizing some verses from the Quran. The teacher gave her until the next day to learn a few verses from a small surah. Lamees spent the entire evening trying to memorize, but her fear of the teacher paralyzed her ability to focus and distracted her concentration, preventing her from memorizing anything. That night, she eventually fell asleep, afraid of the following day, with watery eyes from crying and sadness, despite her mother's attempts to soothe her.

At midnight, my wife woke me up with fear on her face. "Hurry up, it's Lamees." I jumped out of bed and rushed to her room. Lamees was in her bed, reciting the Quran by heart. Her eyes were fixed and unmoving as she stared into space; she wasn't seeing us or feeling our presence, as if she were hypnotized.

Our attempts to get her attention were unsuccessful, as if she were in a trance. She was reading in flawless language, as if she had learned it for years. My wife and I followed along with what she was reading in the Quran. I can assure you that she read many verses and surahs without any mistakes. She read for a long time and didn't stop until sunrise, when she went back to sleep."

"Has she kept all that in her memory?"

The mukhtar laughed: "When she woke up the next day, she denied everything that had happened and did not remember any of it. The teacher punished her again the next day, despite my wife's assurances that she had memorized most of the Quran and that she had heard her reciting. No one believed us, not even Lamees. What do you say about this, Mr. Mamdouh?"

"Though it's strange and uncommon, we can come up with many explanations if we want to go into it."

"Her mother says she was possessed that night. It wasn't she who was reading, but a spirit that possessed her."

"Did it happen again?"

"No, never."

Chapter Nine

It is said that the torment of conscience, depression, and inner psychological conflicts may underlie many physical illnesses, which physical medicine has been unable to identify the causes of and therefore cannot cure. Some believe that these issues are also responsible for many visions and dreams.

I wondered whether the photo had any connection to what happened to Abu Jassim and Abu Anwar or if it revealed the torment of conscience.

I returned to the apartment and examined the camera. I flipped it over and inspected the details of its construction. I was puzzled about where it came from, how my father acquired it, and why he had kept it in a locked box all these years.

Hanan had an important suggestion:

"The only one who might recognize it is my aunt Umm Hassan, who is the only one still alive from that time period. The problem is that she has been ill for a long time, ever since her husband died. She's quite forgetful and is gradually losing her memory. She hardly recognized me the last time I visited her. The doctors say it could be Alzheimer's."

"Well, there won't be any harm in visiting her and seeing how she's doing. I miss her, though."

Zeina and I went to visit my aunt together. It was her first time going out with me. During the taxi ride, she pointed out the sights as if I were a confused tourist.

"Why did you study ancient languages? Isn't it boring?"

"Everyone I know thinks so, but ancient languages are a link to the past, and I am fond of history."

"What do you like about the past and history?"

"I like to know where I come from—my father, my grandfather, and all my ancestors."

"Have you found what you were looking for? Have you learned what you wanted to know?"

I looked at her in amazement and said, "I never thought to ask myself that. Now I realize I got caught up in the details and lost sight of what I was trying to find."

"What do you mean?"

History has taken me in various directions. I have been captivated by events and stories. Did you know that some narratives in history are more beautiful than any fiction or novel ever penned by a writer or even imagined by any author? These are tales crafted by chance and fate, with a beginning but no end, as long as history advances into the future. There are stories about love that are more romantic than any love story or play written by Shakespeare or Victor Hugo. Conversely, there are tales of brutality that are more horrifying and bloody than any nightmare a human can conceive. History is an exhilarating, ongoing narrative that never concludes and does not cease until the end of time."

Zina gazed at me for a long moment, captivated, then asked innocently:

"Are you in love? I burst out laughing: What gave you the idea?"

"I don't know, maybe the way you talk."

"Oh my God, all I needed was you. Isn't your mother's curiosity and questions enough for me?"

"Still, you didn't answer my question. I hope you are. I don't meet real lovers very often these days; I see them only on the screen."

"There are always lovers around us, but it's the fear. The fear of disclosure. Love has always been a critical issue in our society, especially for women. That's why people are cautious; they prefer to keep it in the dark, as if the sun would hurt or burn it."

My aunt Mariam resided with her son Hassan on their farm in Zabadani Resort. The connection between my father and my aunt was particularly strong. Mariam was my father's go-to person, and he was hers, too. He never forgot the effort she put into her seamstress work to support him when he was growing up or how she took care of him as he matured, even after she got married.

I wondered along the way if she would recognize me or if she had any idea about the camera I was carrying.

The farm was situated on a hilltop that overlooked the Zabadani plain.

It was still morning when we arrived. My cousin Hassan was waiting for us as if we had an appointment. Indeed, after he welcomed us and greeted me on my arrival from America, he said:

"My heart was telling me you were coming. Can you believe that?"

"How so?"

"You know that my mother, your aunt, is gradually losing her memory. Day after day, she forgets parts of the present and recalls more of the past. Then she forgets the recent past and remembers the very distant past until she no longer recognizes any of us. But strangely enough, her memory seems to be stuck on her wedding day, and she remembers every detail of that time. She constantly mentions your father. Today, she is in a strange state of nervousness, almost restless. She keeps asking about Ahmed, your father. "Where is Ahmed? Is there any news about Ahmed? When will Ahmed come?" Whenever someone rings the bell, she gets out of bed and asks, "Has Ahmed come?"

I revealed the real reason I came. I told him about the box and the camera, but he didn't have a clue.

"I don't think asking her will help; she doesn't even recognize me, much less you or anything."

We entered her room, where she was lying down, half asleep. Her old age was evident; gray hair covered her head, and weakness and frailty enveloped her body. She opened her eyes when she sensed our presence in the room. Then she looked at us and surveyed our faces. When her gaze fell on me, she smiled broadly, and her eyes shone strangely. I asked her, "Do you remember who I am?" She mumbled unintelligible words. She raised her voice and said, "Why are you late, Ahmed?"

I corrected her, "I'm not Ahmed, I'm Mamdouh, Ahmed's son." She looked at me strangely, then ignored what I said and reached out to Zeina, grabbing her hand and addressing her:

"I've been waiting for you. How are you?"

Zeina stuttered and didn't know what to say.

"I think she's mistaken you for someone else," Hassan said. "Don't worry about what she says; she always confuses people."

"Did you bring me my wedding dress, Ahmed?"

I felt saddened by her memory's weakness. I said, "It will be ready soon."

She suddenly turned to Zeina and asked, "Rose, did you bring the camera with you?"

Her question echoed like an explosion.

"What camera?" I exclaimed eagerly.

She kept chatting with Zeina, who stood there looking puzzled. "Aren't you going to take pictures of me on my wedding day like we planned?"

I swiftly removed the camera from the bag.

"You mean this camera?"

She smiled when she saw it, then turned to Zeina. "Thank you, Rose. After the wedding is over, we'll take some pictures."

She closed her eyes again. Hassan was amazed at what happened and wondered:

"Who is Rose?" asked Hassan

I explained

"She's a French woman my father worked for. Maybe we'll find a photo of her among my aunt's things. I wondered if there were pictures of her at my aunt's wedding. Hassan denied ever having seen such a picture."

"If there were such photos, I would remember them. Anyway, all my mother's personal things are still in her closet. There are many photos, letters, and old things. I'll get them for you." He opened her closet and rummaged through it quietly and carefully:

"She doesn't let anyone go through her things."

Then, out of nowhere, her voice said, "Bring the brown leather bag."

Then she turned to me and said, "It's your bag, Ahmed. Did you come to pick it up?"

Hassan took out an old bag and handed it to my aunt. She straightened up and gestured for me to come closer. I sat beside her on the edge of the bed. She opened the bag, which smelled of old perfumes. She reached in and pulled out its contents: scissors, combs, nail files, old dried nail polish bottles, and empty perfume bottles. There were photos, letters, and old papers that held no value except to the person who kept them. In my mind, suddenly, the salon came alive again; the women's voices were loud and boisterous, and for a moment, I could almost hear Rose and my father whispering and laughing as they worked side by side. Most of the photos featured my aunt, her deceased husband, and her children. One photo was particularly old: my father, my aunt, and several men. My father was the only one wearing a suit and a fez. I asked her:

"Who are they?"

"They are your cousins, have you forgotten them?"

An envelope caught my eye: old, yellowed, and marked by foreign writing. I opened it, only to find it empty, but the handwritten address on the envelope intrigued me.

Mademoiselle Rose Dubonnet

16 Rue Boissy d'anglais, Madeleine, Paris

"It's not a postal letter; I noticed there's no date or stamps, it must be a hand-delivered letter. "

I asked my aunt: "What is this envelope? Where did it come from? Who gave it to you?" But our questions were met with blank stares and silence. She didn't recognize the envelope. It meant nothing to her. Where was the letter inside the envelope, and what did Rose write in it? My aunt didn't provide answers to my questions, but her visit was certainly helpful and gave me a sense of hope that a path had opened for me, one that would lead to the beginning of solving the mystery.

Chapter Ten

"How are you, Mamdouh? Are you okay?"

It was Louise's voice from Los Angeles. She had slipped from my mind amid events, and I had completely forgotten about her to the point where her existence felt strange, as if she were from another planet. I was completely distracted from her, but her voice on the other end restored some of my lost emotional equilibrium. Louise became my last resort, the only one who could help me clear Lamees from my mind and nerves and cleanse my blood of her toxins. I felt the warmth in her voice as she asked how I was doing.

"Are you ok?

"What do you mean?"

"You don't sound quite right."

"I'm fine, why do you say that?"

"I know you from your voice. You're not well."

"Maybe it's because I've been away from you."

"No, you're not fine."

I hesitated a bit before I said it:

"Things have happened."

"Emotional?"

"Why do you say that?"

"You have a sad tone in your voice; are you going through an emotional crisis?"

"Maybe I miss you."

"Hey, you can talk to me about it; I'm your friend, and I'm here to listen to whatever you're going through."

Rest assured, I'm fine; your worries are misplaced.

She was silent for a while, and then she said:

"I know you are there for another woman."

I laughed and said :

"You mean the beach girl? I assure you, I didn't find any girl on the beach waiting for me."

"She is in your heart and your mind."

"You underestimate me."

Anyway, I'm not complaining; I'm content with what you give me. I'll stay by your side as long as you need me. And if you need me now, I'll come right away.

"No, no, no, no need. I assure you, it's not what you think. You know I love you."

She laughed and said, "Thank you."

"Why do you say thank you? You know you mean a lot to me, Louise."

Louise paused for a while, then she said in a voice she tried to keep calm.

"If you choose to come back, I'll be waiting for you. If you choose to stay there, I would understand and won't hold it against you."

"I told you I'll be back soon, rest assured."

I knew I was lying to her, and she knew it too. I can't succeed in deceiving a woman; they read my thoughts and understand the truth of my emotions, no matter how much I try to embellish or cover them up. Is it that obvious that I'm in love with another woman? It's funny how Louise caught me with the very first word. She caught me on the phone, thousands of kilometers across seas and oceans. No matter how cautious or clever I try to be or how many plans I make, I'm exposed in front of them, always betrayed by some verbal slip or emotion, becoming an open book in their hands. I wonder if I talk in my sleep? What did I do that made Louise realize there was another woman? Anyway, yes, there is another woman; I won't deceive myself. There is Lamees, and I love Lamees despite everything she has done and is doing to me. However, I had to make a painful decision about her. I had to distance myself from her completely and repair my relationship with Louise, for the good of both Louise and me.

I don't know why, after the call, I had this feeling that I needed to make that decision as quickly as possible because I was about to transform Louise into a different person, into a predator and a vampire.

I lay there for a long time, thinking about this from every angle. Lamees had taken over all my feelings and thoughts, making it hard to push her out of my heart. Deep down, I really didn't want to, even though I had to. I had to endure a lot of pain to keep from losing my mind and going mad. I needed to take the first step. I finally arrived at that decision.

I called Louise, who was surprised to hear from me and anxiously asked, "Are you okay?"

I asked her:

"Do you like Paris?"

Chapter Eleven

I'm not sure what I would find in Paris. I don't know if Rose's address is still valid. She's supposed to be in her eighties by now. Is she still alive?

I have to go there; something is nagging at me, insisting that the answers I'm seeking are there, at this address, the only relic I have from the past. Rose couldn't have vanished without anyone knowing where she went.

Louise and I agreed to meet in Paris in two days. Paris is the city of love and romance. I hoped to mend my relationship with Louise. This trip to Paris was my chance to rescue myself from drowning in the tumultuous oceans of Lamees.

I decided to travel, set the date, and informed Hanan and the mukhtar.

On the phone, the mukhtar's voice sounded weak. I asked him, "Has there been any new development in the issue of the photo?"

"Nothing new, Abu Jassim doesn't leave the photo for a moment."

"I need the photo and want it with me on my trip."

"I don't think he's giving it to anyone; it's his only hope of seeing again."

"What about Abu Anwar? How is he doing?"

"He's still in a coma. His condition is deteriorating day by day."

His voice on the phone sounded a bit sad. "What's wrong, Abu Hamza? Are you okay?"

"It's Lamees."

I said, terrified, "What's wrong with her?"

"She's sick."

After a moment of self-control, I asked, "How do you know? You told me she doesn't communicate with you."

"She told me herself, she's been sick for two days, she called me. Usually, she doesn't do that unless she's desperate. She considers me her last resort."

"What's wrong with her?"

"I don't know, a nervous breakdown, the doctor says she's depressed, she has a high fever."

He was silent, and I didn't speak up. I was too upset to know what to say.

"She asked about you."

"What? About me?"

"Yes."

I stuttered; I didn't know what to say. I wanted to hang up, to run away. His voice sounded sad when he said:

"She eagerly asked about you."

I wasn't sure what to say.

"Can you please tell me what's going on with her? What's happening to her? You were also sick, so do you two have some issue I'm not aware of?"

"You know, we were together in the same university."

"I remember she went through the same condition when she was in college and nearly lost her life. It occurs to me now that you were there both times. Can you tell me what's going on?"

I no longer have anything to hide about our relationship. After reflecting for a while, I said:

"Do you trust me, Abu Hamza?"

"Yes, I know you're a good guy."

"I certainly don't want to cause you or her any harm."

"I am confident of that."

"Would you wait for me until I return from Paris? I can't tell you anything over the phone right now."

"As you wish."

I felt relieved when I hung up. I needed some time to gather my thoughts and decide what to tell him. How should I tell him? What should I say, considering I don't even know much about my relationship with her? He mentioned that she's been sick for two days, since the incident in her apartment. Could it be that she's sick because of me?

She asked about me. That means she's thinking about me. I don't want to be the cause of her illness again. But what did I do to hurt her? Why should I blame myself for her illness when I'm the one who got sick because of her? She crushed my heart with her fist, and now she complains that her hand hurts? Did the sound of gunfire disturb her when she fired her bullets at my dreams? But yet, what is the secret of this hidden joy that began to beat inside my heart? Is she really sick because of me? Does that mean she's still...?

God, I didn't even want to think about that possibility.

I couldn't help but call her.

A woman's voice spoke to me in French. I assumed it was the voice of the woman in Lamees' bed. I tried to ignore her and asked about Lamees. The female voice said: "I'm Isabelle, you're Mamdouh, aren't you?"

"Yes"

"Lamees is sick, do you know that?"

"Yes."

"She's worried about you. Why don't you answer her calls?"

"I want to talk to her. Now"

"Okay, but she's asleep now. Shall I wake her up?"

"Yes."

I waited for a while, and then Lamees's voice came to me, weak and faint.

"How are you, Mamdouh? They told me you were sick."

"I was a little indisposed, but now I'm fine. How are you?"

"I'm not feeling well. I haven't slept for two nights. I've been thinking about you; you haven't left my mind. Are you still holding a grudge against me?"

I sarcastically said, "Do you mean you wept and shed tears for my sake?"

She laughed and said playfully, "No, not me, there was a whole family of cockroaches crying for you inside my eyes."

I said in a serious voice: "I honestly don't know how I should feel about you anymore. I was devastated that night. I still don't understand what the meaning of all that was."

"I didn't mean to hurt you, but you're an idiot."

"What do you want from me?"

"I want you to love me as much as I love you."

I growled:

"What an insensitive woman you are, I came crawling back to you, I never told anyone in my life I love you as sincerely as I told you, what more did you want?"

"I'm not the same; I've changed a lot. You said it yourself, and it's been a long time."

"I love you just the way you are."

"Does that mean I have to thank you for that? Does that mean I have to fall into your lap right away?"

"Let's give ourselves a new chance."

"You know, she said, I'm starting to feel better, your words have revitalized me."

"How I long to see you now. You know, moments ago, I was hoping to forget you, and now I struggle not to lose you."

She kept silent and didn't answer.

"Why are you silent? What are you thinking about?"

"Would you answer me honestly if I asked you a question?"

"Of course."

"Tell me honestly: Did you enjoy that night with Isabelle?"

I lost my temper and shouted:

"Fuck you, Lamees."

I said that and hung up the phone angrily.

Lamees had become a mystery; I could no longer predict her behavior. Mustafa's words still whispered in my ear.

"My advice to you is to stay away from her and leave her alone."

She is definitely not the Lamees I used to know. Something about her has changed; many things have shifted. There's something unusual going on in her life. Is she serious in her behavior, or is it some kind of joke I'm not familiar with? Another issue is, what should I tell Abu Hamza when he asks me about her and my relationship with her? What can I say to him?

Either way, I won't kid myself; I've lost my ability to fight back. I'm not a salmon that swims and jumps against the current. I can't withstand the fierce waves in Lamees' ocean anymore. I used to love being tossed about by the waves and washed ashore with broken ribs. I would return and throw myself between its folds with joy and pleasure, despite the pain and the blood flowing from my wounds.

There is a virus that has undoubtedly infected me, and I can't get rid of it. I try to cure it, but it's no use. This virus is incurable; its name is Lamees. It has infiltrated my nerves, my brain, and my dreams, and I can't eradicate it.

It frustrates me that despite everything she's done to me, I'm more drawn to her than ever. What bothers me even more is that my anger is manifesting in fantasies and visions where I imagine raping Lamees over and over, while she's there, laughing and looking at me with a triumphant expression. Where does this anger towards her come from, and why do I find myself lusting after her more intensely each time? It feels like I've lost my footing, and I'm lost with her, while she's become this mercurial force that's impossible to grasp. The fear of losing her forever is driving me crazy. I've been constantly asking myself, "Is she genuine or is she manipulating me?" But I want her, flaws and all – whether it's the Lamees with her tenderness and warmth or the Lamees with her cunning and mystery. She has me under her spell, and I'm helpless, waiting for her to strike at any moment.

Chapter Twelve

Who says we can only have sex with the person we love? I don't know, but I can confidently say it's nonsense. I can come up with endless stories of people who have had sex with all kinds of living things, even animals, and I don't think they ever fell in love with them.

And whoever claims that this only applies to men and that women surrender only to the ones they love is spreading nonsense. The restrictions placed on women may have been stricter, but our history is, however, filled with stories of women who sought sex for pleasure. These women were so beautiful and powerful that they subtly defied social constraints.

I ignored Lamees's incessant calls; she must be worried, but I didn't care anymore. I wanted her to worry and agonize like I do now.

Eventually, she gave up and sent me a short text message:

"Don't evade the truth; you didn't answer my question. Did you have fun that night? Did you ask yourself who you were making love to, Louise or Isabelle?"

Poor Louise, what's her fault in all this? What did I get myself into? Why didn't I just walk away and leave Lamees alone like Mustafa suggested? Lucky Mustafa; he found someone to help him escape from her. But I wonder if he survived—did he make it out alive?

I boarded the plane, determined to start my life anew. I genuinely resolved to forget Lamees and look forward to Paris, where my relationship with Louise would continue.

Louise had gone ahead of me and was already in Paris, where she would meet me at the airport.

I decided to be hers, body and soul.

I felt comfortable with this decision and convinced myself that Louise and Paris were the best remedy for my condition.

The airplane was half full, and I was sitting by the window. An old man occupied the seat next to the aisle, with an empty seat between us. The plane took off for a night flight lasting about six hours. We were served food, and then the lights were turned off for those who wanted to close their eyes and rest their nerves.

Traveling at night profoundly affects me, leaving a peculiar emotional impact. I remember being on a night flight, with pitch darkness outside the plane despite the clear, cloudless sky. At times, I could see the lights of small towns or villages far below, and I would follow those lights until they vanished. I rested my head against the window and gazed into the darkness outside the airplane. There was no sign of life on the ground. This continued for a long while until a small light appeared in the distance below. A light that would hardly capture anyone's attention—a solitary light resembling a small star lost in the black sky, easily overlooked and ignored. I envisioned the light coming from a small, isolated house with a father, mother, and children playing, enjoying life. Cut off from the world, their presence went unnoticed. I pictured a little child among them, standing at the window, gazing at the sky, searching for a dream, or maybe a vision. He caught a glimpse of a distant airplane, unnoticed and unheeded by those on the ground. He imagined himself on that plane and relished it, and suddenly my gaze met his; he smiled at me, and I smiled back. He waved at me as tears streamed down my face. I couldn't stop crying. I sobbed silently, unnoticed in the darkness of the plane. I still don't know why.

A brunette flight attendant approached and whispered a few words in the man's ear. He got up from his seat and followed her toward the front of the plane to first class. I closed my eyes, savoring the fact that I had the whole place to myself. It wasn't until I fell asleep that I felt someone sit down next to me. A female hand touched mine, and when I opened my eyes, it was Isabelle.

She looked at me, smiled, and said in a French accent:

"Hello, Mamdouh. Do you remember me? I'm Isabelle." She approached me and kissed me on the cheek, as if I were her childhood friend. "Does it bother you if I sit next to you? The guy sitting next to me is very annoying."

She didn't wait for my answer; she just relaxed in the seat and continued.

"He's been trying to harass me since I got on the plane."

I laughed, "The poor guy doesn't realize he's harassing a vampire."

"Don't exaggerate, Mamdouh, I'm glad I found you."

She stopped talking suddenly and looked at me with clear blue eyes:

"Do you think I'm vulgar?"

"What do you mean?"

"You spoke to me harshly on the phone."

"How was I supposed to react to what you did?"

"I thought we had a good time. You were great. I, too, was great, we enjoyed it, right?"

"Please don't mention that night."

"Anyway, don't make a big deal out of it. Tell me, what do you have in Paris? Tourism or business?" I answered tersely: "Neither, it's private."

I fell silent and looked out the airplane window. She glanced at me and said, "You can be nice and ask me how I'm doing, it's better than looking at the black space outside."

"So, what do you have in France?" I asked

She smiled and said excitedly:

"I'm going to see my daughter; I miss her so much."

"So you're married?"

"I was once. But not now. My daughter lives with her father in Lyon."

"Have you been on a visit to Syria?"

"I'm working there at the university temporarily with Lamees. I teach French."

"In addition to your other job?"

"What job?"

"Cannibalism."

Isabelle laughed and waved her hand, implying that I was exaggerating too much.

However, Isabelle was nice. I reexamined her features again. I hadn't had a chance the last time she was in bed to check her out. I was too traumatized. She was a blonde in her early forties—beautiful even without any makeup, not even lipstick. A smile never left her lips, showcasing soft curves and a gentle nose. Her body was slender, making her look much younger than her actual age. Her tight skirt noticeably accentuated her legs.

"I won't bother you at all. She rested her head on my shoulder and closed her eyes; you can go back to sleep."

The scent of her hair and perfume wafted into my nostrils, keeping me from falling asleep. I couldn't resist sneaking a glance at her legs. When she noticed that, she remarked harshly without lifting her head:

"It looks like I'm keeping you from sleeping."

"No."

She lifted her head and gazed into my eyes: "You're lusting after me now, aren't you?"

"No."

"Not even a little bit?"

"No."

"You're a liar and a hypocrite, too. Don't you want to put your hand on my leg and caress it, feel its softness? especially when we're alone, out of sight, and everyone else is asleep."

"Maybe it may cross my mind, but that doesn't mean I'd do it."

"Why not? What's stopping you?"

She took my hand and placed it quietly on her knee. I tried to pull it back, but she squeezed it and kept it there with her hand on top of mine. After a moment of silence, she said: "Do you start to feel them?"

"What?"

"The hormones, can you feel them flowing through your body? The Testosterones, they will incite sexual images and fantasies that will occupy your mind and thoughts."

She looked at me like a scientist examining a mouse in a lab experiment, and I observed her curiously.

Now I can feel your heartbeat increasing. It's adrenaline rushing through your blood, causing your breathing to quicken, and your lust fever is gradually rising.

My hand immediately withdrew. She spoke with frustration: "Don't you realize that right now, with the plane floating in space, in this vast universe, we're just two tiny, insignificant people - we're nothing but nobodies in this huge world. Yet, we could have so much happiness, so much pleasure if we wanted to. What do you think's holding us back from grabbing this precious chance?"

I didn't answer; I kept staring into her eyes, fixed on mine as my temperature began to rise.

She continued: "They are words, words in our minds, words that are nothing more than a collection of letters, to which we have given meaningless meanings, such as loyalty, friendship, love, and many, many words that we have shaped into shapeless forms. Then we worshipped them. We became fearful of them. We forgot that they are just words, and in the end, they will remain words in our minds. But what's more dangerous is that we neglected what's more important. Do you know what's more important?"

I did not answer.

"You and I. Look at how we look at each other from a distance, distressed that we can't touch each other or extend a bridge between our souls through our fingers. What does it matter to the whole world if there are two beings like us, somewhere, at some moment, embracing each other tenderly? I assure you that no one in the universe cares about what we do. And if we don't do it now, if we miss the moment, we will be the only losers when we leave the airplane. And I'm sorry to tell you that we lose a lot at every moment of our lives. We lose so much because we cannot put these words out of our minds. My hand had unconsciously rested on her knee as I listened to her words. But when I realized that she had finished speaking, I calmly withdrew my hand and said sarcastically:

"Is this a sermon, or what?"

"Ah, what an idiot you are. I thought you were smarter than that."

"Do you say that to all the men you want to seduce?"

Isabelle laughed

"Do you think I need this sermon, as you called it, to get the man I want?" Isabelle asked for a blanket from the hostess. She covered herself and her legs and smiled slyly. "That's better, now you can sleep."

"You're really evil."

She laughed: "Now you can close your eyes."

But I didn't, because I couldn't sleep anymore. I sat silently, motionless so as not to disturb her. The plane was calm and quiet, and most passengers were either asleep or staring at the screen in front of them. She took a black blindfold out of her bag and handed it to me:

"Put it over your eyes, it will help you sleep." I put the blindfold on and closed my eyes.

After a while, she got up and whispered, "I'm going to the restroom. Don't run away." Without taking off the blindfold, I said, "I don't think they will let me out of the airplane."

She came back a little later. I sensed her sit quietly, trying not to disturb me, and she rested her head on my shoulder. It was quiet for a while, and I was about to fall asleep when I felt her hand slide under the blanket to my knee and rest on it. I didn't move, but her hand started moving forward towards my private parts, so I grabbed her and pushed her away, preventing her from continuing. I tried to remove the blindfold, and she whispered in my ear: "Close your eyes and relax. You'd better calm down, you're going to draw attention to us." I sat motionless with my eyes closed. Her fingers gripping my belt. She whispered in a soft voice: "You desire my body, and I want you. Why bother to resist?"

I lost my ability to resist as her hands fiddled with my clothes, and her lips nibbled on mine. But I noticed that the perfume smelled different. It wasn't Isabelle's perfume. I quickly lifted the blindfold, realizing that Lamees was the woman next to me.

"Surprise?" Lamees said, laughing. I turned around and looked for Isabelle.

"Are you searching for Isabelle?"

But Isabelle wasn't there.

I don't remember if I said anything; the words had vanished. The surprise was overwhelming. I quickly straightened my clothes while Lamees quietly got up, smiling at me. She stood silently in the hallway and walked toward the bathroom. Suddenly, she turned around, returned to me in my seat, leaned over, gave me a serious look, and whispered, her smile gone: "Who's more appealing, Lamees or Isabelle?"

"What are you doing? What do you want from me?"

"What do you think I would want from you?"

"I don't know, you tell me."

"I want you to be happy."

She looked at me for a long time. She seemed like she wanted to add something, but she turned her face and continued walking toward the bathroom, then disappeared inside. After a while, the old man returned and sat down. I waited a little longer for Lamees to return, but she didn't. She was taking too long in the bathroom, and the plane was starting to land. I went to the bathroom to look for her. She had already come out. I asked the flight attendant about her, but she didn't recognize her. I also inquired about Isabelle, the blonde Frenchwoman, but to no avail.

"In first class, there are two women who match the description you provided, but you have to wait for the plane to land".

After the flight attendant insisted, I returned to my seat and reluctantly sat down, almost losing my mind. My thoughts were a whirlwind of questions. What is the relationship between Lamees and Isabelle? What does she mean by "I want you to be happy?" How can I be happy? What do I want from her?

The plane landed at Charles de Gaulle Airport. I rushed to the first-class cabin as soon as it stopped, but the passengers had already left. I got off the plane looking for them in the corners of the airport, in the hallways, in the bathrooms, by the luggage, and finally I spotted them heading towards the exit door. I ran towards them, dragging my suitcase. When they saw me heading towards them, they stopped and waved at me. They were smiling a few feet away from me, and I was about to shout their names when Louise appeared.

Louise was beaming with joy and looking her best. Tears filled her eyes when she hugged me and kissed me as she lingered in my arms. I felt confused and wasn't in the mood to feign joy, yet I returned her hug and kiss while Lamees and Isabelle watched from a distance. I pretended to be happy to see her, trying to mask any signs of anxiety and discomfort. Louise was ecstatic; her gloomy expression was gone, replaced by pure joy, as if she had a new lease on life. She bounced around like a little girl in a playground. As we waited for the metro to the center of Paris, she spoke excitedly, not concealing her happiness that we were together in Paris, the city of love and passion. Once we boarded the metro, Lamees and Isabelle stood a few steps away from me, as if we were strangers. Lamees was watching us, likely surprised by Louise's presence. For the first time, when our gazes met, I recognized in her eyes the Lamees I had known in the past.

A great sadness came over me. I don't know why.

At that moment, I felt pity for Louise and pity for myself.

Chapter Thirteen

Finding Rose's address was a significant milestone that greatly boosted my storyline. But as they say, finding the path is not the same as walking it. Locating the light switch in a dark room doesn't necessarily mean eliminating the darkness, because if it's too bright, the light can be more blinding than the darkness itself.

We arrived in Paris.

The French accordion began to play.

Paris has a special charm; it's unique. It has a virus that everyone who visits, especially for the first time, catches: the virus of love. On our way to the hotel, Louise asked me, "What is the first thing we will do in Paris?"

I thought for a while and started giving her suggestions:

Eiffel Tower? Louvre? Seine River tour? Champs-Elysees? Arc de Triomphe?

"I promised myself," she said, "that we would stroll on the "Pont Neuf" over the Seine and hug and kiss you in the moonlight."

"Your romance makes me feel ashamed of myself."

"Why?" she said in surprise.

"Because I promised myself that I would attend an erotic, sexually explicit show with you on Pigalle Street."

She gazed at me with the wonder of a naive little girl and said:

"Can we really do that?"

"Of course, why else would they have invented Paris?"

I dropped my suitcase at the hotel, and we quickly set off for our first night together. We took the metro to Rue Pigalle. There was the "Moulin Rouge," but it was a bit more upscale than I had envisioned. I wasn't looking for a show; I was seeking something unusual. We entered a small club. The receptionist at the door explained to me that the shows were very special.

He didn't lie.

The shows were so scandalous that I was shocked by what they offered. The sexual practices were taking place in front of us, steps away from our table. The lighting was only on the stage, sparing the onlookers from embarrassment. Most of the audience was made up of American tourists who watched the show as casually as if they were watching the news. Louise, on the other hand, sat glued to me, watching in amazement, but she couldn't hide her enjoyment of what she was seeing, although she sometimes tried to hide a shy laugh, sometimes grabbed my hand and squeezed it, hid her head behind my back or covered her eyes with her palms. Every time I look at her, I catch a glimpse of Lamees when she was in college, exploring the secrets of sex and the pleasures of love together. We didn't feel the time pass as the shows kept coming; we were mesmerized by what was being offered until I looked at the watch, and it was after three in the morning. We reluctantly left the place while the show was still going on.

As we walked out into the street, a cold chill enveloped us, making it feel like we had entered a different world.

Louise's only comment was: "I don't know how they can do that in public".

I said, "I think we should ask: What makes us desire to watch them do it? Did it bother you to attend the show?"

She smiled shyly, then laughed and said, "I can't hide the fact that I enjoyed it very much."

"Now it's your turn to fulfill your wishes, let's go. "

We took a taxi to the "Pont Neuf." When we got off, Louise was thrilled and seemed to be in another world of magic and romance. The charm of the place overwhelmed her. She stood looking at the Seine while holding my arm with both hands. The bridge was one of the most popular spots for lovers. Despite the late hour, it was crowded with tourists, painters, florists, and a few instrumentalists.

"Has your dream come true now?" I said, looking at her enchanted eyes

"One thing remains." She hugged me in the middle of the crowd and planted a passionate kiss on my lips.

We went back to the hotel. Our tour on the first day surely paid off, and Paris made a big impression on Louise. We made love in the hotel all night, only stopping for breakfast, and she kept asking for more. Her image began to blend in my mind with that of Lamees, to the point that I sometimes pictured myself in Lamees's arms instead of Louise's. Maybe that's what kept me going all day. We didn't sleep until the afternoon when we were exhausted.

For the first time since we met, she fell asleep hugging me. I could feel her tears soaking my chest.

The next morning, I woke up late; Louise wasn't there. She had left me a note saying she had gone out shopping and wouldn't be late. When she returned, she was loaded with bags from brands like Galeries Lafayette and Spring. She said, delighted:

"This is the first thing a woman is supposed to do in Paris."

She emptied the bags filled with clothes and began trying them on in front of me, piece by piece, acting like a fashion model.

We continued our tour of Paris, going up the Eiffel Tower, visiting the Latin Quarter, and hanging out in bars and cafes. We took a boat ride on the Seine, visited the Louvre, and strolled down the Champs-Élysées.

We asked the waiter to bring us a dish representing traditional French cuisine in a restaurant. The waiter was delighted by this request and left, only to return with two plates of escargot. He stated that this dish is the pride of French cuisine. Louise was shocked and couldn't hide her disgust. She even forbade me from taking a single bite out of curiosity. The waiter, frustrated, smiled in disappointment as he lifted the two plates and treated us with contempt as he brought us American hamburgers instead. But Louise had lost her appetite. Back at the hotel that night, Louise suddenly asked me, her face beaming with happiness:

"What really inspired you to make this trip to Paris?"

"Isn't it better than visiting your psychiatrist?"

"Tell me the truth. I know you, I can't believe you're bringing me to Paris out of romance."

"Why do you always question my motives? "

She laughed: "I don't trust you or your motives."

"How ungrateful you are. Is this how you thank me?"

"On the contrary, I am more than grateful to you; I have never been so happy in my entire life. But there must be a reason behind this invitation. I will not deceive myself by saying that you have brought me to kneel before you at the feet of the Eiffel Tower and give me a wedding ring."

"God, you're such a blackmailer."

"I learned that from you. I'm your creation."

"If that's true, then I'll have to remake you. It looks like I made a monster out of you by mistake."

She snarled and growled like a lioness, but I continued

"I won't lie to you; in fact, there is a great deal of truth in some of what you have said. There's another reason I came to Paris."

I told her about Rose. She listened very carefully and intently. She was so moved that she cried. Louise found it so romantic; she said with tears in her eyes:

"You come all this way after all this time to look for your father's sweetheart?" She kissed me and thanked me.

"I didn't think you were so affectionate," she remarked.

She gave me the feeling she was grateful to me. I don't know why, as if the story meant more to her than to me. I discovered how sensitive and emotional she is. Most importantly, I realized the vast gap between her and Lamees. It was like the difference between the innocence of a child and the debauchery of a whore.

But the thing is, my heart was beating for the whore.

Louise was eager to reach the end of the story. The following day, we embarked on our quest to solve the mystery.

I had no idea what a surprise awaited me.

We took a taxi. I gave the chauffeur the address I had. He had no trouble finding it; it was a small street behind the Champs-Élysées.

Building number 16 was in the center of the street. Unfortunately, it was a large building with several floors, and the address didn't specify which floor. We stood at its entrance, confused, with no one to ask.

A few meters away from the building stood a small bar and café. I entered with Louise, and the bartender greeted us warmly; it was an unusual welcome. He was so friendly that he began talking to me as if he knew me. He led us to a table, served us coffee, and entertained me with news about people I didn't know. My French couldn't keep up with him, so I spoke to him in English. He looked surprised and laughed. I asked him why he was laughing. He laughed more, pointed to Louise, and said in English that I was playing dumb in front of her. Louise looked at me and asked if I knew the man. I said no. We couldn't find a reason for his strange behavior. I handed him the paper with the address, and as soon as he read it, he burst out laughing and called the waitress. He spoke to her while pointing at me and then showed her the paper. She gave it a quick glance, looked at us in surprise, and laughed too.

Louise and I exchanged glances, unable to comprehend anything. I apologized for the embarrassment I had caused her:

"The address seems to be out of date or doesn't exist." Finally, the waiter pulled out a pen and wrote on the paper: Fifth floor, apartment 10. He handed it to me, patting me on the shoulder and laughing. It felt like I had told him a good joke.

I was annoyed with him and wondered why he was laughing. Louise was also upset and found his behavior to be rude and inconsistent with the renowned French etiquette.

We entered the building; it was very old, almost ancient, with offices and apartments. The elevator was also outdated. We reached the fifth floor, stood in front of apartment 10, and rang the doorbell.

A woman in her fifties opened the door. She looked at me, shocked, and froze momentarily as she stared. Then, she let out a shriek of fear and slammed the door in our faces. Louise and I stood, puzzled and terrified, in front of the closed door, wondering what had happened and how we had alarmed her.

Seconds later, the door opened again, and it was a surprise. A big surprise, I couldn't believe my eyes, Louise gasped in astonishment. The person who opened the door was I. I was standing face to face with myself. If it weren't for the different clothes, I would have thought I was looking at my reflection in the mirror. Same face, same nose, same eyes, same features, same proportions, same height; even the hairstyle was almost identical. We stood there, looking at each other. I felt amazed, but the other me remained calm. After a moment, the surprised expression on his face faded and was replaced by a very friendly smile. He said, as if he had been waiting for me forever:

"Here you are at last."

He extended his hand and said, "Hi, I can't believe it." I held my hand out, but he pulled me toward him and hugged me. I stood there like a statue, unsure of what to do, and when he looked at me again, there was a tear in his eye. Louise, like me, remained still, glancing between us with her mouth agape.

"You're Mamdouh, aren't you?"

I was shocked by the question. Louise gasped again. I nodded in agreement. I looked at him, my mind racing, searching for answers.

The puzzle was big, but the answer was more straightforward than I imagined. He took me by the hand, let me in, and continued walking until we reached a large salon. He went to a wall with a large picture on it. "Look," he said, it was a picture similar to the one I had seen at my aunt's house, showing my father, aunt, and husband. With a slight difference, this picture shows my father, my aunt, and a young girl. It was taken on the same day and in the same place because the clothes were the same. He pointed his finger at the picture of my father and said, "This is my father, Ahmed, and this is my aunt Maryam." I looked at the photo in amazement.

"This is a picture of my father and aunt. How did it come here?"

"Rose de Bonnet brought it here."

He pointed to the beautiful girl in the photo, who resembles a Hollywood actress, and continued with a big smile.

"She is my mother, Rose de Bonnet." Then he extended his hand again toward me and said

"As for me, my name is: François Ahmed Sawaf."

"What?"

"Yes, I'm your brother". He continued laughing, "Your big brother."

I extended my hand towards him. "I am Mamdouh Ahmed Sawaf."

He hugged me again. There was so much love in his embrace. Louise's eyes filled with tears as she wiped them away. The joy on François's face was extraordinary.

I exclaimed in amazement, "As if you were waiting for me, did you know about me before?"

"Believe me, I didn't know you existed before this moment. I was as surprised by you as you were by me."

"But how? I don't understand. It's like you were expecting me."

"My mom told me, "One day someone will knock on this door. Someone will ask about me. Wait for him and be ready. He could be your father or someone from his side. She would never let me change the apartment or sell it. This address was the only hope for you to find us. I waited for this day all my life. I always dreamed of my father, and I dreamed of this day, the day I would meet someone I belonged to and who belonged to me. But I never expected that person to be my little brother. Imagine that our father's blood runs through our veins and we carry his genes. Is he still alive?

Unfortunately, no, he passed away more than twenty years ago. But how did you know my name?

"I guessed it because my father, Ahmed, as my mother told me, was called Abu Mamdouh."

"That's true. But honestly, we didn't know there was a relationship between Rose and Ahmed; no one knew he had a son. All we knew was that Ahmed worked for Rose at the salon, then left the salon and traveled to Lebanon for an unknown reason."

I was silent for a while, then asked hesitantly: "And Rose, is she still...?"

"Yes, she is alive, but she is weak and sick. Only hope has kept her alive all these years. She searched for you extensively and left her address everywhere she looked, but Ahmed vanished without a trace, which worried my mother. She feared that something had happened to him. Nevertheless, she continued to wait for him and remained faithful to him. She loved him deeply, and I will let her share her story with Ahmed; she will be overjoyed when I tell her the news."

François asked anxiously:

"Do you have pictures of him?"

"Yes, but if you look in the mirror, you will see him; you and I are mirror images of him. I took some photos out of my bag and showed them to him. He looked at them joyfully as if he had found a treasure.

We spent most of the evening looking at the photos and answering his questions about some people. "

"Who's that?" he asked, pointing to a little girl standing next to me in one of the photos.

"That's Hanan, our sister."

"My sister? Hanan? My sister."

He pronounced the name and repeated it with happiness shining in his eyes and glowing in his gaze.

"Yes, and she has a daughter named Zeina, who is sixteen years old."

"That means I'm also an uncle. I can't believe what is happening to me. A few minutes ago, I was alone with no one in the world but my mother, and now I have a family, relatives, and a girl who will call me Uncle François. I feel like I have a real sense of belonging now. Suddenly, he looked at Louise as if he hadn't noticed her before, and I rushed to introduce her:

"This is Louise; she's my friend from California, where I've lived for a long time. He kissed her hand and apologized profusely, then asked me if I was married, and I said no."

"And you?" I asked. "Are you married?"

"I was once, but we divorced a long time ago. I don't think about it anymore. I don't want to leave my mom alone."

"But where is Rose now?"

"She spends her days in Nice. We have a villa there. The weather in Paris doesn't suit her well. We'll go tomorrow, but tonight we're celebrating."

As we left the building, we passed by the bar. I told François what had happened. He was so excited that he deliberately walked into the bar and greeted the bartender and waitress, who stood stunned, glancing back and forth between us without saying a word.

We laughed so much that night—the three of us. We ate dinner at a fancy restaurant overlooking the Eiffel Tower at the Trocadero. He asked if we'd like to try the French specialty, but Louise insisted on steak and fries.

"In France, you shouldn't miss the opportunity to taste French dishes."

Louise said in an apologetic and complimentary tone:

"I love French food, but my stomach hasn't gotten used to it and needs some time." During the meal, Louise was perfectly in tune with François, conversing at her own pace while he listened intently. She shared the story of how we met in America, talked about her work, and then discussed my job as a lecturer in ancient languages. François shared details about his work at the software company he owns. Then suddenly, he told me in classical Arabic: "Do you know that I can speak Arabic, a little bit?" I was shocked and amazed to hear him speak Syrian traditional Arabic.

"My mother made me learn it from a young age because it is my father's language."

"Your mother is a wonderful woman, I can't wait to meet her."

By the end of the evening, Louise was calm and quiet, listening and deep in thought. She had drunk more than usual but never took her eyes off François and listened intently. When we left the restaurant, François rejected the idea of staying at the hotel and insisted that we move our things out and settle in the apartment because it was spacious and had room for everyone.

Louise didn't sleep all night, and she wasn't eager to have sex. Something was on her mind, but she refused to say it. She was not the same Louise who had spent the first night with me in Paris.

When I woke up in the morning, she was not in bed; she was in the living room, fully dressed and waiting for us to wake up.

During breakfast, she looked exhausted, but that didn't stop her from chatting with François while avoiding eye contact with me. Maybe she's just tired, I thought, but I sensed something deeper was going on.

Chapter Fourteen

I heard a song by Charles Aznavour:

The walls of my life are so smooth

I try to cling to them, but I can't

I find myself slipping towards my inevitable fate:

"death by love"

The drive to Nice was enjoyable, especially as we crossed the beautiful and picturesque French countryside. I sat next to François, and we chatted the whole way. Louise sat alone in the back at her request. She remained silent, never engaging in any conversation.

We only stopped once for a break and a cup of coffee along the way.

We arrived at the villa at noon. It was on a high hill overlooking the sea.

When the car stopped at the door, a woman came out to greet us and led us directly to a large terrace overlooking a forest that sloped down to the beach. There, an old woman over seventy sat in a rocking chair, asleep. We quietly took seats next to her, trying not to make any noise. But François approached her, kissed her on the forehead, and whispered in her ear: "Look who I brought you."

Rose opened her eyes and looked around slowly and lazily. First, she saw Louise, then she turned to me and started gazing at me, then looked at François again, and back at me. Finally, my presence piqued her interest. She adjusted her seat, bringing her face closer to mine. She glanced at François once more, as if she couldn't believe what she was seeing. Then she opened her mouth to let out a suppressed scream and said in a weary voice:

"Unbelievable! Who are you? Ahmed? you can't be Ahmed, you're too young to be Ahmed."

"I am Mamdouh, Ahmed's son."

"He's my brother," François exclaimed excitedly.

"Oh my God! Is it possible?"

Rose looked at me, then opened her arms and said, "Come here, come here, come into my arms." She hugged me, held my head, and kissed my hair and forehead.

"Finally, you came; finally, Ahmed became real. There were times when I doubted myself, when I realized that my story with him was nothing but a dream. I feared I would die in doubt, lost between dream and reality. Are you really real?

"Yes"

"And your father, Ahmed, what about him?"

"Unfortunately, he died twenty years ago. We never knew about you, except what he told us."

"What did he tell you?"

"That he worked for you for a while, then left for Beirut. He said he learned his techniques from you. But he never told us—my mother, sister, or me—about his relationship with you. He never talked about you in his life except once, when he mentioned you accidentally and briefly, and told us how he came to know you when he was selling raspberries."

Rose laughed at the mention of raspberries, got up from her seat, leaned on François, and walked over to the garden balcony.

"Look," she said, pointing to a tree in the garden's center. "My raspberry tree is fifty years old; I planted it here just to remind me of him. Now tell me, where were you living? I spent a lot of time looking for him. He left before he knew I was pregnant; I wanted to tell him, but he disappeared. No one knew anything about him, not even his sister."

"He went to Beirut, where he met and married my mother. The only time he returned to Damascus, he died. I took a tie with a golden soaring eagle from my bag and showed it to her.

"He kept this tie all his life for special occasions and died wearing it".

Rose grasped the tie with a hesitant, trembling hand, unable to believe what was happening before her, as if the distant past had suddenly reappeared. She smiled, and her eyes filled with tears. She hugged the tie and said, "So he hasn't forgotten me either."

She looked at the tree and said, after calming herself down a bit:

"When I sit here, on the balcony facing the tree, Syria lies far beyond the horizon. I never grow tired or bored of gazing at it. It's as if I see him. I have come to die here, close to the raspberry tree, surrounded by cacti, and in front of me in the distance, beyond the horizon, the specter of Syria and the specter of Ahmed."

"I don't think he forgot you for a moment either; he was always far away from us, immersed in his loneliness and thoughts. We didn't know what was going on in his mind, but now I can guess that you were always with him and that he was thinking about you all the time. But it makes me wonder about the nature of the relationship between the two of you: what happened, and why did you part ways? Did you have a fight?"

Rose laughed and said disapprovingly, "No, no, never, he was the kindest person I've ever known, and if I could give my life to him, I would. Because he once did."

"You're making me more and more curious," I said longingly.

"I'm also curious about your story with Ahmed," Louise said.

Chapter Fifteen

I sometimes wonder if consciousness is a part of the energy that exploded at the beginning of the universe.

Has this consciousness been fragmented in the same way as the energy?

Is it so dispersed, diffused, and distributed throughout creation that our individual consciousness represents only a tiny fraction of the total consciousness?

If this is true, then our memory must store in our brains a long history, the history of all humanity. Perhaps even further back, so that if we were to go back in time, we would reach that first moment,

the decisive moment,

The starting point.

Rose said:

It all began on a warm spring morning in 1940. It had been less than a year since I arrived in Damascus with Philippe, a French officer in the Vichy forces, whom I loved and cherished, and we were almost engaged to be married. Philippe was a handsome, cheerful young man whom I loved at first sight, but he was unstable in his work. He often went on missions, leaving me alone. However, that didn't trouble me because I knew that no matter how long he was gone, he would return to me. I loved him deeply, as I had no one else in this new country. At the time, I was twenty years old and very beautiful—one of the most stunning women. Since childhood, I had nurtured a passion for beauty, so I opened a salon in one of Damascus's most prestigious neighborhoods to occupy my time while he was away. The finest women of Damascus, both French and Syrian, frequented my salon for their makeup.

One morning, while I was working, I heard a voice in the street. I didn't understand what it was saying, so I looked out the window and saw a fifteen-year-old boy. I went out to him, and he rushed over to offer me his goods. He was carrying small baskets of local berries. He gave me one, I tasted it, and I liked it; I hadn't known it before, and it was a strange fruit to me. I let him into the salon, bought the berries, and fed them to my customers, who enjoyed them. I noticed his curiosity and fascination, so I let him rest for a while. He was dressed in Damascene garb: a kumbaz. He looked calm and shy, polite and soft-spoken.

I was kind to him, tipped him, and asked him to bring me more berries every week.

He would come and sit in a corner of the salon, observing our work with curiosity and interest. He was smart and witty, often trying to be helpful while in the shop. He cleaned the floor, wiped the tools, polished the mirrors, and stood next to me, holding tools like a doctor's assistant in an operating room. He possessed great energy and an impressive ability to learn the language. Whenever he held a tool, he would show it to me, and I would say its name in French. He would memorize it and repeat it, enabling him to easily learn a lot of work-related vocabulary and some expressions, which made our communication much smoother.

A few weeks went by, and the berry season came to a close. For him, the berries were merely an excuse to visit, while for me, they represented an opportunity to give him some money. However, the spark in his eyes when he was next to me suggested that being in the shop with me meant more to him than money.

He came in late spring with the last basket of berries and looked sad, saying it was a gift from him because it marked the end of the season. At the time, I didn't understand what he meant; I didn't realize it suggested he wouldn't be able to come anymore. So, I didn't pay much attention to how troubled he seemed when he left the store that evening. I was going through a rough patch in my relationship with

Philippe, and we were constantly fighting. He would make excuses to cancel our plans or find ways to go out with his friends, which often left me upset and anxious.

Ahmed didn't show up the following week. I asked Janet, my Syrian assistant, and she informed me it was to be expected since the berry season had ended. I replied nervously and without thinking, "That doesn't mean he shouldn't show up." Two days later, at the end of a long, tiring day, Ahmed entered the shop smiling, carrying a basket, but there were no berries in it.

I interrupted, smiling: " he brought you cactus fruit instead." Rose laughed and said:

"So you know the story of the cactus. I was in a hurry that day. Philippe and I had a date, and I was doing my makeup while waiting for him to come. I grabbed a cactus in my hand without realizing it."

Rose looked at her hands as if it were happening right now, and then recounted the incident with the cactus and how it was the reason Ahmed joined the salon. Louise listened as if it were one of Scheherazade's stories. Rose continued: I discovered during that period that he had a good sense of humor, manners, and quick wit.

He brought a joyful atmosphere to the shop. He was a humorist who could make me laugh at any time, and he could skillfully imitate anyone with his movements and voice. Whenever I felt angry or sad for some reason, he would do anything to please me, imitating my gait, movements, and tone of voice in a way that made me laugh. In less than two years, Ahmed became a handsome and confident young man and became my right-hand man in the shop after my assistant Gil left and returned to France. By that time, he had mastered the French language to some extent, so I could communicate with him easily.

Syria was under the French Vichy government. In 1941, we received news that the Allies had begun their plan to take Syria and Lebanon from the Axis powers. The battles were intense, with Allied forces from Britain, Australia, and the Free French advancing toward Syria and Lebanon from Palestine in the south—specifically toward Daraa and Al-Laytani, and from Iraq in the east, heading toward Palmyra. Airplanes from both sides participated in these battles. We heard about the significant battle that took place over Homs, which was one of the fiercest air skirmishes, where Allied Tomahawks inflicted heavy losses on the Vichy forces' aircraft, managing to destroy dozens of planes at the airport in Homs in mere seconds. The Allies emerged victorious and entered Damascus in late June 1941. Philippe had joined the Free French and was away for long stretches under the pretext of military missions. I missed him and felt lonely until Charles de Gaulle visited Damascus on July 25th of that year. People came out to welcome him, including Syrians, especially after he promised them independence.

Philippe had promised to take me to see him and greet him, and I was excited and ready for it. However, Philippe apologized at the last minute because he had to run an errand in Daraa, south of Syria. I was very disappointed. Knowing how unhappy I was, Ahmed suggested that De Gaulle would be in Beirut tomorrow. He will tour the streets; "you can see him there." I liked the idea. I looked at him and simply said, "Then you will take me there."

"But I don't know Beirut and I've never been there."

"I'll manage, don't worry, I just want someone with me, I want you to go with me." Ahmed was happy and excited, not because he was going to see Charles de Gaulle, which meant nothing to him, but because it was the first time he was leaving Damascus. In addition to that, he was going to have me with him. Through the salon, I had gotten to know most of the French officials' wives. One of them offered to take us with her in a government car, and I agreed. The next day, I wore my best suit, and Ahmed couldn't have been happier, sitting in the black diplomatic car next to the driver while I sat in the back with the official's wife. In Beirut, my friend left us in the city center to return and pick us up in the evening for our return to Damascus. People filled the streets, and neither of us knew anything about Beirut. We were told that de Gaulle's motorcade would pass by the seaside, so we took the tram to the Manara area by the sea, then walked along the Corniche. We enjoyed the view of the sea. I felt happy; the sea breeze refreshed me, and I forgot my anger at Philippe. Ahmed, in his tuxedo and red fez, was walking, looking at the sea for the first time in his life. He appeared confused, sometimes walking in front of me, next to me, or behind me, talking excitedly, pointing with his hands, losing himself in the crowd, so we almost lost each other more than once.

I had to hold his hand to avoid getting lost in the chaos.

I didn't realize that it wasn't normal for him to hold his hand. I didn't know it would mean as much to him as it did. It must have been a big event for him because he suddenly calmed down, became silent, and didn't care about anything.

Eventually, the procession passed, I waved to Charles de Gaulle, and the celebration was over.

We had to spend the rest of the day waiting for my friend to return and pick us up, so we decided to go to the beach. We sat on the rocks watching the fishermen and dipped our feet in the water. Afterward, we took a walk to search for shells and collected them along the way. He told me about his sisters and the neighborhood; I discovered that he loves poetry and secretly writes it, memorizing it instead of putting it down on paper. He read me a poem in Arabic; I didn't understand it, but the music was clear. He said it describes the tree at their house, with its branches, fruits, and birds' nest. He talked about how it gives him a sense of comfort and security. I found the poem naive, yet I couldn't help but admire this new side of his personality.

We entered a large, upscale restaurant that overlooked the sea.

We ate, rested from our walk, and were about to leave when I suddenly heard a familiar voice and a laugh in a corner of the restaurant that was not unknown to me: It was undoubtedly Philippe's voice. I happily turned in the direction of the voice; it was indeed Philippe. The big shock was that he was not alone; a beautiful young girl accompanied him, and they were sitting next to each other, his arm around her shoulder and feeding her.

I couldn't believe my eyes. I could feel the fire burning inside me, and I tried to control myself. I was confused: what should I do? How should I behave? I was about to pull away when he kissed her, and that's when I lost my mind. I headed toward Philippe's table while Ahmed stayed there, surprised by my sudden, strange behavior. Philippe was shocked to see me standing in front of him like a ghost from sudden death. Confused, as if he had seen a demon, he quickly pulled his arm away from the girl and greeted me with a pale smile. He introduced her to me as an old friend. But I didn't give him a chance to continue lying; I grabbed his plate of food and threw its contents in his face. Philippe stood up, his expression changed, and his face grew angry.

"What are you doing, you despicable girl?"

I didn't like how he said the word "despicable." I couldn't help but slap him and say:

"You are the despicable one, you asshole."

I left quickly, almost choking, and stepped into the open air before bursting into tears. I walked for over an hour, lost in thought, with images of him feeding her, sipping wine from her glass, and kissing her replaying in my mind. My anger and spite escalated. By the time I came to my senses, the sun was about to set, and I found myself sitting on the beach in front of Raouche Rock. I had completely forgotten about Ahmed, who stood behind me, silent and sullen, looking at me with confusion.

"Let's go meet my friend and go back."

"It was a sad end to Ahmed's first trip," Rose spoke in a low voice while sharing her story, trying to remain calm. However, she was thoroughly agitated by the time she reached this point, as if the event were still fresh in her mind.

"You can rest now, François said, you've had enough for today."

"The events are happening in my mind as if they happened yesterday, and I want you and Mamdouh to know them because they are part of your past."

I said, "I think you should rest today. We will continue tomorrow."

François provided us with a room featuring a sea view and encouraged us to relax for the evening before going out for dinner at a restaurant in Nice. Louise opted to stay in the garden since she wasn't tired. She appeared to be in a bad mood, perhaps due to Rose's story. As for me, as soon as I rested my head on the pillow, I fell asleep. Louise's voice woke me up:

"Get up. It's time to go to the restaurant."

"What time is it?"

"It's after ten o'clock."

I got up groggily while Louise searched her clothes for a dress suitable for the occasion. She hummed happily and admired herself in the dress, making dance moves as she did so.

"Why did you let me sleep until now?"

"We weren't here; François took me on a tour around Nice, and we just got back. Come on, get up, we have to go."

I didn't comment, but I was annoyed. I felt like she deliberately excluded me.

We went out to dinner. Louise sat next to François in the car while I sat in the back. She looked visibly happy and relieved.

François said it was a restaurant near the flower market in the city center:

This restaurant serves traditional French food. What would you like to eat?

"I don't know, what do you suggest?"

"Of course, there's seafood, there's meat, there's cheese, what would you like, Louise?

"I'll take what you take."

"Maybe you won't like it, I'll have a plate of escargot."

Remembering her previous attitude, I smiled at her, but she replied without thinking.

"OK, I take the same as you."

I looked at her in surprise, but she avoided my gaze, blushing. I asked her incredulously, "Are you sure this is what you want?"

"Yes. She said firmly without looking at me."

"Well then, I'll have the same as you."

François smiled pleasantly and said, "You will like this dish. It's a French tradition."

I was never the type to refuse any kind of food; I always loved to experiment, and my motto about food was, "Eat anything that someone else can eat and survive." I could eat anything if I had to, but I didn't expect Louise to finish her plate. She was watching François eat and imitating him, and he was encouraging her. However, she didn't need any encouragement; she devoured everything on her plate. At first, she took a sip of wine after each bite, but after a while, she started eating normally. I looked at her in wonder, but all the while, she avoided my gaze. On the way back, Louise asked François, "I wonder if Rose is sober now?"

"I don't know, why do you ask?"

"If she's awake, I'd love for her to continue her story. I'm dying to know what happened."

Rose was indeed awake. She called us to her room and asked how we were doing and how our evening was going. Louise couldn't help but ask if she could continue her story because she couldn't wait until morning. Rose smiled and said, as she straightened up in bed, "I'm excited about the rest of the story too, so come on, sit down."

I said, "There's something I want to show you before you continue your story.

"What is it?"

"A camera."

She was shocked, as if an electric current had touched her. She said fearfully, "A Camera?" I calmly replied, "Yes, a camera. Wait a bit; don't start before I come back." I went to my bag, took out the camera, and rushed back with it. I approached her and showed it to her. I didn't need to ask if it was the same camera. The fear in her eyes as she stared at it told me the answer.

"I thought it was out of my life forever," she said, "but here it is, back on my deathbed. But how did it get to you? Where did you find it?"

It was buried in the front yard of the house; it is the reason I came to France.

She looked at me and asked in astonishment:

"But how did you manage to hold it? Only Ahmed could touch it." I briefly told her what happened, from discovering the box in the garden to taking the miraculous photo. François exclaimed in amazement: "You say that the watch is moving inside the picture. I can't believe it. Where is the picture now?""

"It's still in Damascus; Abu Jassim is using it as a means of sight."

"That's the strangest thing I've ever heard."

After some hesitation, Rose took the camera and felt it with her fingers, muttering: ""So it wasn't the camera itself. The issue was inside the camera, in the photo.""

I asked her: "What's its story, what's its secret?"

Rose responded: "The camera may be ordinary, but what happened because of it is extraordinary."

Chapter Sixteen

I often hesitate before writing or expressing love. It's not as easy to talk about it as one might think. Revealing your emotions to others and making them empathize with you is challenging. Unlike discussing sex, where your style doesn't matter, it's always interesting and captivating. Writing about love those delicate sensations and the agony of anticipation and longing—is much riskier. A writer must possess considerable skill and craftsmanship to touch the reader's senses and emotions; they need artistry to engage their words, controlling feelings and allowing readers to experience the tenderness of separation and endure the bitterness of memories. By nature, we dislike human weakness and emotional pleading because these evoke ridicule, disgust, and perhaps nausea.

We sat around Rose's bed, while François sat on the bed. Rose said

"The day after we returned from Beirut, I wasn't feeling well. I couldn't work. It was Ahmed who ended up doing all the work I was supposed to do.

He was worried, observing my behavior from a distance while I avoided his gaze. Thus, I stayed silent all day and the following day as well.

Since nothing had happened over the past two days, and since Philippe didn't show up, my anger subsided, but it was replaced by fear. I began to regret my behavior toward Philippe and felt that I had overreacted and should have given him room to apologize. I started making excuses for what he had done, as I was sure he loved me and would come back to me.

After a few days of his absence, I was very worried that something must have happened to him.

Things didn't go as I expected. He was supposed to show up and apologize; I rejects his apology. He gets down on one knee and cries. I give in to his pleas and forgive him, and then he hugs me, kisses me, and makes up for his offense.

But none of this happened. Philippe didn't show up.

I loved him; I had no one else. I was terrified that he had left me forever. I began asking my friends about him and any news they had. I left messages at all the places he frequented, asking him to call me. But there was no sign of him, which only added to my frustration.

One day, a friend hurriedly told me he was at a café with a group of friends, so I left the store and went to see him. He was already there, laughing and drinking with his friends. The place felt like a bar, and when I walked in, I was met with shouts of admiration and invitations from various tables offering me glasses of wine. I expected Philippe to throw himself into my arms, but he turned his face away from me. I stood near his table, waiting for him to turn around and welcome me. He ignored me. It was an embarrassing situation, but I didn't care. I wanted him and didn't want to lose him. I said in a reproachful tone, "How are you, Philippe? Is this how you greet me?" But he didn't answer, didn't turn around, and pretended not to care, so I continued:

"I came to apologize for what I did the other day." He didn't answer and kept talking to his neighbor as if I weren't there. I said:

"I understand now that you may have had an excuse."

He didn't answer; he just looked at me coldly and continued drinking from the glass in his hand. His companions were winking and whispering.

"Please, forgive me. I reached out to him with tears in my eyes, 'Don't leave me, I need you.'" Everyone in the café fell silent, and all eyes were on me.

"Don't give up on me, please, I would do anything for you to forgive me." He remained silent, fidgeting in his chair. Finally, he turned to me, smiled, and nudged a chair with his leg, gesturing for me to sit down. And so we were back together again, but not without a rift in our relationship. The wound inside me was too deep.

Since then, I've started to doubt my relationship with Philippe, and I keep asking myself: "Did Philippe actually come back to me?"

The answer became clear to me in a negative way through his indifferent and irresponsible behavior. I learned about his numerous affairs from clients, and he was notorious for his many female escapades.

I was the last to learn about them; in fact, I tried to avoid finding out. I realized I was deceiving myself, but my pride prevented me from accepting the harsh truth. I remained confident in my beauty and my ability to win him back at any moment.

On the other hand, there was Ahmed. He was handsome but had no romantic aspirations, and I never heard him talk about any girls. Perhaps this was due to his conservative upbringing. The doors of pleasure were wide open for him. As a seventeen-year-old working all day with women, especially aristocratic ones, he could have had many adventures. However, he showed no interest in them, though he sometimes jokingly hinted at the attempts of some to seduce him or win his affection. Nevertheless, he was careful not to go too far with any of them. I didn't know then if he acted this way to protect the store's reputation or to spare my feelings. My relationship with him was strange and complicated, and his behavior toward me fluctuated. When customers were in the store, he would joke with me and act relaxed. But when there was no work to do and we were alone in the shop, he became extremely shy and silent. He would hide near a window, watching the street and not saying a word to me. I used to be annoyed by his silence, so I would throw something at him and say:

"What's wrong with you today, Ahmed? Did the cat swallow your tongue?"

He would turn to me, smile, and not answer, sometimes not even daring to look at me, until I sometimes thought he was afraid of me.

As for his sisters Mariam and Salma, I got to know them later, when his younger sister got married. She was sixteen years old. A few days before her wedding, Ahmed came to me and said shyly:

"Salma asked me to ask you to do her a favor".

I looked at him in surprise and said:

"Salma?"

"Yes, my sister Salma, she is asking if you would be willing to do her makeup on her wedding night?"

He didn't hear me say yes, so he continued, embarrassed: "Of course, I told her that you don't have time and that you are busy."

"I said yes, ok, I'll do it".

"What? Are you going to do it? Do the makeup to her?"

"Yes, of course? I'd love to, I'd love to see where you and your sisters live."

"It's a very modest house in the Bab Srijeh neighborhood."

Rose looked at us at the mention of Bab Srijeh, closed her eyes, and took a deep breath.

The smell of this neighborhood still fills my chest. A scent that is a strange mixture: perfumery shops, laurel soap mingling with the aroma of freshly baked bread, and the scent of cheeses. It's as if I were walking through a neighborhood of a thousand nights and one. The magic of the place was so overwhelming that I didn't notice the strange looks from people who were surprised to see me there. I walked with my new assistant, Janet, while Ahmed, wearing his red fez, led us, deliberately taking a few steps ahead and hurrying to avoid embarrassment. We entered a narrow lane barely wide enough for more than two people, with old houses on both sides, and I could hear women whispering and catch a glimpse of their figures behind the high windows. Finally, we reached the house, which was an old and small residence, nothing like the grand homes of Damascus I had visited before.

His sister Mariam welcomed us, but did not allow Ahmed to enter because the house was full of women, and none of the men were permitted inside.

So, Ahmed left us and went away on the condition that he would come back to pick us up after the wedding.

I was amazed by the joy and happiness that characterized the women during the process of decorating the bride and practicing their rituals. They danced, sang, played the Tabla, and let out exotic sounds of joy. It was an unforgettable evening. We all laughed and danced. Then it was my turn to decorate the bride, and all the women and girls joined in. The bride was so beautiful; she and Maryam cried tears of joy. The bride wore a white wedding dress and was ready. As soon as we finished, the groom's sister and her mother came and took the bride with them to her new home, where the groom was waiting for her, and the wedding ceremonies would take place.

At the end of the wedding, Ahmed came to pick us up in a horse-drawn carriage he had rented. He dropped his sister off at home and then took Janet to her house in Bab Touma. Finally, he drove me home. It was after midnight, and my apartment was above the shop on Abu Rummana Street. Ahmed sat in the front seat next to the carriage driver while I remained alone in the back. The streets were empty, and the sound of the horse's hooves echoed in the distance. The events of the party and wedding replayed in my mind, with echoes of music, singing, and dancing filling my senses. I was so happy that I wished the night would last forever and that the party would never end. When the carriage reached Beirut Street along the banks of the Barada River, I couldn't resist the magic of the moment; I asked Ahmed if we could walk the distance, and he reluctantly agreed, noting it was cold at night. We walked side by side. A French police patrol on horseback passed us on the other side of the street. As usual, Ahmed kept a bit of distance between us. It was clear he was confused; he would occasionally overtake me, prompting me to ask him to slow down a little. He complied, but then he would accidentally speed up again. I decided to put an end to his hesitation. I stopped suddenly, and he halted as well, looking at me in wonder: "Come on, give me your hand. Come on, hold my hand." I don't forget his face at that moment and how he blushed, but I took his hand and slipped my arm under his armpit, saying firmly, "Now we can walk." We strolled in silence for a few moments, enjoying the view of the river with the streetlights shimmering on its surface, while listening to the gurgling water. Meanwhile, Ahmed was sweating. I told him about the wedding and how happy I was to be there, then asked him about his sister Mariam and why she wasn't married yet. He explained how she had suffered a lot as the eldest and dedicated herself to raising him and his sister, learning to sew and working at home to support them.

I suddenly asked him: "When will you get married?" Surprised by the question, he said quickly and shyly: "Not yet."

"Why? Is there a girl waiting for you? Maybe you would like to marry her."

He was confused and stammered, but he answered that he was not thinking about marriage at all, not until Maryam got married. Then he added, as if to clarify something:

"Anyway, no girl is waiting for me."

We continued walking, and I put my hand in his coat pocket when I felt cold. He smiled shyly without looking at me.

"How's your poetry? Are you still writing poems?"

He smiled and said, "I wrote a new one."

"Really? What's it about?"

"About the sea."

"I wish I could understand Arabic to hear it from you. So you liked the sea?"

"Very much, it's beautiful and scary at the same time."

"Read me some verses, even if they're in Arabic."

Ahmed read the poem; his accent differed from the previous one, and his voice was soft and sweet.

"It's a beautiful poem, though I didn't understand a word."

"So, how do you know it's beautiful?"

"From the sound of your voice."

On the way, I sang. I was feeling happy and free. At that time, there was a new song by Edith Piaf called

"La vie en rose." I loved that song, and I still do. I started singing it:

"When he takes me in his arms and speaks softly in my ears

Life becomes rosy

He whispers words of love to me,

words of everyday, that mean a lot to me.

He came into my life and became a part of my happiness.

He is mine, and I am his, for life,

He has sworn it to me."

I was singing, and Ahmed listened in silence. When I reached the part where it says: "When he takes me in his arms and whispers words of love to me, life becomes rosy," I was in tears, and my voice was betraying me. But he didn't notice. I sang the whole way, and he listened silently, smiling.

After that night, Ahmed changed. He viewed me differently.

After that night, he became quieter, less playful, and more introspective. He would sit for long periods, gazing out the window, and I sometimes caught him stealing glances at me—observing me work or peeking at me through the mirror, looking worried and overwhelmed. I noticed that he was becoming more invested in me. My feminine instincts told me there was something deeper than respect and appreciation in this boy's heart for me.

I felt he was in love with me.

I liked that; it didn't surprise me too much. Ahmed wasn't the first man to fall in love with me; every man, without exception, has fallen for me at first sight. They've all been willing to go to great lengths to please me. I liked the idea of Ahmed being in love with me. It satisfied my ego that he ignored all the young girls who sought his heart just to fall for me, even though he's several years younger than I am.

Ahmed had gotten to know Philippe through the latter's frequent visits to the shop to take me to the officers' club parties or the theater.

On those occasions, Philippe and I were always the center of attention. I could see that all the girls and women envied me for having this young, handsome officer with his charming looks and sweet smile, while the men wished they were in his place. He would sometimes visit me at the shop, and I would leave when he arrived to go up to my apartment. Ahmed never once asked me about him or tried to investigate my relationship with him. However, I sensed that he was annoyed by Philippe's visits and how he treated me. Philippe was condescending and arrogant, and perhaps part of his arrogance stemmed from the fact that he completely had me charmed. But what bothered Ahmed the most was that Philippe came up to the apartment with me.

But anyway, this relationship had to end. It wasn't a balanced relationship from the start, and I was foolish to let it continue for so long. One day, Janet came to tell me that Philippe had been injured and was in the hospital. I was so scared and terrified; I didn't know what to do. Ahmed offered to accompany me, and he made sure to calm me down along the way.

When we arrived at the hospital, they showed us to his room, and there was a surprise. Philippe lay on the bed with his wounds bandaged. A very elegant Frenchman stood at the bedside, a woman sat in a chair next to him, and at the edge of the bed sat a beautiful young girl who appeared to be their daughter. Philippe was not pleased to see us. He greeted us in a strange manner. He ignored me and welcomed Ahmed as if he were a good friend, quickly introducing him to the man, who turned out to be the French High Commissioner and his wife, and then continued hesitantly:

"And this is their daughter Colette, my fiancée."

The news was like a thunderbolt. Philippe was sweating, and he was right to be afraid of me. because I was about to say something foolish if Ahmed hadn't intervened. Ahmed surprised us all when he introduced me: "This is Rose Dupont, my fiancée."

It was a second shock, but I didn't comment on it. I just smiled, a faint smile. I extended my hand to Colette, the ground nearly shook beneath my feet, and I felt the heat burning in my face and head. It was a tough time in the hospital, and I remained silent the entire time while Philippe explained to us how he was injured during training, avoiding looking at me. I almost felt like I was going to explode, but then Ahmed asked for permission to leave. He wished Philippe well, and we departed. I didn't look Philippe in the eye when we left, and Philippe didn't look at me either.

We walked out of the hospital and back to the shop. We didn't say a word the entire way. I was in tears. I felt angry, frustrated, devastated, and ashamed of myself and Ahmed. However, my shame for Ahmed suddenly transformed into anger that far surpassed my feelings toward Philippe. As soon as we entered the store, I asked Janet to leave. When she left, the volcano inside me erupted, unleashing its fury on poor Ahmed:

"What did you do? How could you degrade me like that? Who are you to consider me your fiancée?" Ahmed wasn't surprised. He expected this attack, so he didn't answer. He was embarrassed and tried to justify his behavior and apologize, but my anger overtook him:

"Who do you think you are? Why did you embarrass me in front of them? Who asked you to behave like this?"

I cursed at him and pushed him, but he remained silent, accepting my insults with patience and subservience. This only fueled my anger further, and I found myself slapping him across the face. Ahmed didn't move or respond to my attack, but the expression on his face shifted, and the look in his eyes changed.

I burst into tears, left the store, and went up to my room immediately. It was one of the darkest days of my life; the world was crumbling before my eyes, the ground was shaking beneath me, and I felt like I had lost my balance. I had never planned for such a situation. I blamed myself for being foolish. I already knew a lot about Philippe and his adventures, but I thought he would tire of them and return to me in the end, and I would have him all to myself. The cruelest part was that the girl in the hospital wasn't a fling; she was his fiancée. This made me despise myself and feel like a plaything he was with until he found the right girl for him.

I stayed in the apartment all day. The next day, I decided to go out; I needed to see people, but not Ahmed. Besides, I had lost my desire to work and even to live. I didn't know where to go; all my friends knew about my relationship with Philippe, and I didn't want to see the gloating or pity on their faces. So, I began wandering the streets alone, without a specific destination. I headed toward Abu Rummana Street and then Salhiya, soon finding myself in Al-Marjeh Square. I continued walking along the bank of the Barada on my way back home, moving aimlessly without a particular goal. The crowd comforted me; the faces and gazes of people pulled me back to reality, easing my pain and giving me hope. I sat on one of the benches and spent hours watching the flowing water, losing myself as I replayed in my mind the stages of my relationship with Philippe and the shameful situations I had put myself in. The most annoying thing was Ahmed's pitying glances. Finally, the sun went down. The street became empty.

Suddenly, I spotted Ahmed and Janet in front of me.

"Thank God you're here, said Janet, We looked everywhere for you and asked all your friends. Ahmed expected to find you here."

I didn't answer, I just looked at Ahmed. He was standing in silence. Janet continued:

"What's wrong? Are you okay? "

"I'm fine. Let go of me."

"You have to be strong, Philippe will recover, God willing, and get out of the hospital and return to you."

Obviously, Ahmed did not tell her anything. I turned to Ahmed, who was pretending to look at the river and avoiding looking at me.

"I told you I'm fine. Leave me, please."

I asked Janet to leave, but she insisted on staying with me. I violently admonished her, and she bowed to my will and left, amazed at my behavior. Ahmed didn't go and stayed with me. We walked together toward the house, silent and distant. Suddenly, he approached me and said in a pleading voice:

"Are you still angry with me? I only meant to spare you the embarrassment. I never meant to offend you."

"You should have stood by me and let me expose him before them; I should have punished him and taken revenge. But you helped him get away with it."

He was silent for a while and then answered me quietly and hesitantly:

"What would you have said to them? How would you have introduced yourself? Would you have told them: I am his mistress?"

His answer shocked me and was more than I could bear; his words made my heart ache, pressing on my wound violently and twisting my nerves. I couldn't control myself; I yelled at him, slapped him in the face, and pushed him away with such force that he nearly fell over.

"Shut up, you despicable boy, you're no better than him, you're even worse than him."

"Why do you say that? You know I would do anything to please you."

"That's right, you're willing to do anything to get me."

"What are you saying?"

"You know what I mean."

Ahmed looked at me with frustration and said:

"Please don't continue, you're angry, you don't know what you're saying."

But I shot him a sharp look and said with resentment:

"I know exactly what I'm saying, yes, I know you want me, I'm not stupid, I can see it in your eyes and gaze. I know you are secretly peeping at me and secretly lusting after me. You are the one who should be asking yourself who you are to me. Have you forgotten yourself? Have you forgotten who you are? Go back to your kumbaz, your neighborhood, your baskets of berries."

I left him standing there, stunned and shocked. I continued to walk impulsively, reveling in the pleasure, the pleasure of revenge. The temple was collapsing around me and the people I loved, but I didn't care anymore.

I reached the house, knowing Ahmed was walking behind me. I turned to him and said, "Don't ever go back to the store. I don't want to see you again."

Ahmed didn't show up the next day. Janet asked me about him, but I didn't answer. I left the shop because I couldn't bear to stay within the walls anymore. Janet was left alone to do all the work, grumbling and taking her anger out on Ahmed and his absence. The next day, Ahmed didn't show up either. I blamed myself, felt very bad about his absence, and waited for him to show up all day.

Two days later, Ahmed arrived early, parked his bicycle at the shop's door, and waited. He didn't open the shop as he usually did, despite having the keys; he was simply waiting for me to come in. I was glad he was back and felt a vague sense of joy, but I didn't show it and didn't pay him any attention. I opened the shop, and he quietly walked in behind me. We resumed our work as if nothing had happened. Janet didn't hide her pleasure at seeing him, but reproached him for not coming the past two days. Ahmed didn't respond or explain his absence. He took a jasmine collar from his pocket and placed it on the chair where I usually work. I ignored it and didn't touch it. I sat by the window all day. Everyone was unusually quiet and seemed tense and nervous. This continued for a few days, and every morning, Ahmed would bring the jasmine collar and place it on the chair next to the old one. He wouldn't let Janet touch it.

I waited for the jasmine collar every morning, not daring to touch it until he left the store. I loved smelling it and wearing it around my neck.

One day, there was an unexpected surprise.

I was at the window as usual when I caught a glimpse of Philippe. I couldn't believe my eyes; he was walking toward the shop. I screamed with joy. For a moment, I forgot what he had done to me, as if I had lost my memory. I rushed to open the door for him, and Philippe entered, laughing as usual, carrying a bouquet of red roses as if nothing had happened. His head was still bandaged. I was about to throw myself into his arms, but I hesitated. I stood there, looking at him happily, but he ignored me and went directly to Ahmed, who was painting a customer's nails. He greeted him warmly, hugged him, and thanked him for saving him from his predicament at the hospital. Ahmed gave him a friendly smile as he gently pushed him away and continued his work.

Finally, Philippe turned to me and opened his arms. I couldn't resist and rushed to him; he kissed me hungrily and held me close.

"You will always be my one big love."

"And Colette?"

"I can't love her more than you, consider her as part of my work, imposed relationships, purely professional relationships."

I looked at Ahmed as if to say, "Did you see how he came back to me?"

But he stared at me with a look of sadness and disappointment. Philippe took my hand and walked toward the door, pulling me along behind him.

"Let's go upstairs." My eyes fell on the mirror and I looked at myself being dragged. I was like a dog being pulled by its master. I despised myself and stopped walking.

It suddenly occurred to me that this wasn't really what I wanted.

I hesitated and looked at Ahmed with fear. He, too, looked at me pleadingly.

"Come on, Philippe said, squeezing my hand and pulling me towards the door."

I hesitated and tried to stop myself and resist him, but, as if hypnotized, I found myself walking without thinking or will.

My gazes were fixed on Ahmed. Suddenly, I heard Ahmed's voice saying in a quiet, shy voice:

"Don't go with him, Rose."

Those were the most beautiful words of love I had ever heard.

His words were a surprise, words I never expected to come out of Ahmed's mouth.

Philippe, who had opened the door with one hand and held my arm with the other, was taken aback by Ahmed's words. He froze; his facial expressions changed, and the smile on his lips vanished. Janet ceased working, and everyone else stood still.

"What did you say?" Philippe asked, surprised. But Ahmed didn't look at him; his eyes were fixed on me.

I looked at him with tears starting to blur my vision: "Why, what's it to you?"

He said: "Don't do it, don't let him ruin your life, you deserve so much better than this. You deserve the best man in the world; you deserve better than him."

Phillip looked stunned and listened in disbelief to what Ahmed was saying. He let go of my hand and calmly walked over to him with a wry smile. He grabbed him by the collar of his shirt and punched him in the face, knocking him to the ground. The clients screamed and retreated to a corner of the store. Ahmed got up, wiping the blood from his mouth. He looked at me and repeatedly said:

"Don't go. Don't let him treat you like this."

Phillip punched him again, pushed him to the ground, and kicked him in the face, stomach, and all over his body while Ahmed kept repeating:

"Don't go."

I was watching the scene, stunned and unable to react. I felt myself drowning while the people around me indifferently watched me suffocate.

Ahmed's hand was the only one reaching out to pick me up. I hesitated, I wanted to grab it tightly, but I was afraid, not for myself but for him, I was scared that he would drown with me.

Philippe pulled me violently toward the door while Ahmed lazily got up, glanced at me, and continued as if he were still following our conversation.

"Yes, everything you said earlier is true. I won't deny it anymore. But you have to leave him, not for my sake, but for yours." Then he looked at Philippe and said

"Don't treat her like that. She is better than any woman you know."

Ahmed was voicing what I didn't dare to admit even to myself. I released Philippe's hand and stood there, staring at Ahmed as if seeing him for the first time. Philippe became enraged and lunged at Ahmed, but this time, Ahmed intercepted him and pushed him away. Philippe drew his gun and aimed it at Ahmed's head, sparks flying from his eyes. I was terrified for Ahmed; I couldn't remain still.

At that moment, there was only me and Ahmed in the universe. I had to decide; I had to hold Ahmed's hand. Either we would survive together, or we would drown together. I blocked the gun and stood between him and Ahmed, panting with fear.

"Move away," Philippe said.

"That's enough, Philippe, get away from him and leave."

"Step back. I have to discipline him. I will make him an example to others."

"If you want to shoot him, the bullet will only reach him through me."

When he saw the determination in my eyes, he stepped back and lowered his gun:

"You should have taught him not to interfere in our affairs. I will leave him in your honor."

He walked toward the door, waving his gun in the air, then turned to me and said,

"I'll be back tomorrow, and it's better not to see him here."

I said in a firm and calm voice

"It's better if you don't come back here at all."

Philippe was shocked: "Are you kicking me out, Rose?"

"I don't want to see you here ever again."

I took the bouquet, placed it in his hands, and quietly walked back towards Ahmed.

As I did so, a new sensation that I had never experienced before swept over me. I felt like I had floated on the water's surface, my face was out into the air, and I took a deep breath that filled my lungs and my life.

Philippe stood at the door for a moment, considering my words. Then he threw the flowers on the ground, stepped on them, and walked out without saying a word. The customers rushed out of the store. Janet and I were the only ones left. I turned to Ahmed, who was staggering behind me with blood running down his face. I said, "you are crazy, what did you do? Did you want to get us killed?"

He laughed, pain showing on his face, as he said, "No, you are the crazy one, you're the one who was going to get the bullet, your body was protecting me."

Then he asked, "Would you really have sacrificed your life for me?"

I didn't know how to respond, and I couldn't even look him in the eye; I wasn't sure what my gaze would convey. He said, "Thank you for saving my life."

"It was you who saved me, despite all the offenses I had committed against you."

"I couldn't stay away from you."

"You poor thing, did you mean what you said? Do you love me that much?"

"Who doesn't? Yes, I love you. I'm not ashamed to tell you now; I've loved you since the first time I laid eyes on you when you came out of the salon door asking me about the berries. Your love taught me to write poetry, real poetry. You were the peaceful tree and the furious sea in my poems. I don't care if you don't love me; someone out there is better than Philippe and me, and it won't be long before you find and love him."

My voice was stifled as I whispered with teary eyes, "Am I really so foolish as to search for that man while he's in my arms?"

I kissed his bloody lips. "You are my hero and my knight."

At that moment, Louise was crying. Her handkerchiefs were no longer enough to wipe away her tears. François looked at me with a smile and said, "How can you not want me to love my father?" Every time I hear this story from my mother, I admire him more and wish I had known him.

I told him with deep sadness that all of this surprises me and makes me feel guilty because, even though I lived with him for a long time, it's now clear to me that I never really knew him.

"After this incident, my life changed," Rose continued. "I suddenly realized that Ahmed was the one I was looking for; he had been in front of me all the time, but I didn't see him."

I loved him passionately. We decided to get married, but we had to wait until his sister Mariam's wedding because Ahmed had vowed not to marry before her wedding.

"And did Maryam get married?"

"Yes"

Louise then asked curiously, "So what happened? How did you two part ways? Rose looked into the distance and flew high, then came back to us and said:

"It's the camera".

Chapter Seventeen

Memory is a peculiar thing. It's an accumulation of events in full detail. The details make one marvel at their accuracy and the way they are stored. When you run into someone and they introduce themselves, you sharpen your memory and review dozens of faces, vainly recalling the moments meant to remind you of them; their face gets lost in the flow and accumulation of so many years, days, hours, and seconds. Suddenly, a faint odor of unknown origin brings the entire event back to your mind, and you relive it as if it happened yesterday. We seem to be trying to forget; our nerves can't handle the burden of history. Our memory attempts to hide what it can out of mercy, and we go along with it, telling ourselves we have forgotten. We don't try to remember for fear of unearthing a painful memory that our subconscious has been trying to protect us from.

We all watched Rose, eager to learn the story of the camera:

One day, a friend who had just returned from Paris came to visit me with this camera, which was very modern at the time, and offered to take some pictures for us. I liked it so much that I proposed buying it.

It was a wonderful thing back then. We used it to take pictures of ourselves in the shop and at Ahmed's house. Mariam liked it so much that she suggested we take photos of her on her wedding night in her bridal dress.

The wedding day was a significant event.

Unexplainable events happened that day, and I still cannot explain them.

On the morning of the wedding day, I gave Ahmed this tie as a gift. He told me that he also had a present for me and would give it to me after the wedding.

The plan was for me to stay with the bride after the wedding party ended and the guests had left, and then Ahmed would come with the camera so we could celebrate together and take pictures to commemorate the occasion. Everything started off well; the wedding took place in Bab Srijeh, at the groom's house, not far from Ahmed's place. It reminded me of his younger sister's wedding. Maryam, the bride, was beautiful, and the wedding was a typical traditional Damascene affair, where the women sang and danced to oriental music, and I joined them while wrapping a shawl around my waist. I laughed a lot and felt very happy. Then the groom arrived, accompanied by a traditional Shamiya parade, as the women sang to welcome him;

he sat next to Maryam. In her white dress, she almost glowed with joy, and then the women began to leave until only the bride, the groom, his mother, and I remained. We prepared dinner and waited for Ahmed to arrive. But Ahmed didn't show up. We waited and waited, but nothing changed. I felt embarrassed to be with the bride and groom on their wedding night. The groom sent someone to look for him, but it was in vain. I was worried because this wasn't like Ahmed. The groom and some of his friends left to search the nearby neighborhoods and beyond. They were gone for a long time and returned without Ahmed. There was no sign of him; I was terrified and uneasy about his disappearance. I feared something bad had happened to him. The men went out again for another round of searching. However, I couldn't wait for news; I had a feeling he was in serious trouble. I didn't know why, but I felt he needed my help. I imagined him drowning and reaching out for assistance.

Despite Mariam's insistence that I stay, I also chose to go out and search for him.

No woman should be alone on the street at this hour, but I didn't care. Mariam lent me her black velvet coat, and I wrapped a shawl around my head to cover my face before stepping outside, even as she pleaded with me to stay and wait.

I had no idea about the neighborhoods of Bab Srijeh. I stepped out of the small, narrow lane by the house onto the main street. The main covered souq street is a long thoroughfare stretching for quite a distance; all the shops were closed, and darkness enveloped the area. I walked blindly, tears streaming down my cheeks. My footsteps echoed on the tiles of the street, breaking the silence and stillness of the place. With no one around, I didn't know where to look or whom to ask.

Eventually, I came to a mosque. I heard the sound of men's voices. I stood at the door, waiting for someone to come out, shivering from the cold and fear. A boy about ten years old emerged, surprised to find me at the mosque's entrance.

I asked him about Ahmed, describing him, his clothes, and his fez. I knew he didn't understand a single French word I was saying. But the boy looked at me quietly and listened intently, then smiled and pointed his finger somewhere inside a lane in the market, saying words I didn't understand. He saw the confusion in my eyes, walked a few steps, then turned to me and gestured for me to follow him. We came to a narrow, dark alley. He stood and pointed at it before taking off running.

I stood at the corner of the alley, trying to figure out what was inside, but it was so dark that you could hardly see your finger. I searched for the boy to call for help, but he had gotten far away and reached the end of the souq. I heard his voice from a distance; he said a few words that echoed in the empty souq and continued to point his finger toward the alley as if urging me to enter it.

I slowly stepped into the darkness of the narrow lane and groped my way until my eyes adjusted to the gloom. The lane had many turns and seemed to stretch on endlessly. On both sides stood the closed doors of old houses, silent and lifeless, as if deserted. I could only hear the sounds of my panting and heartbeat, and I was afraid to continue. Suddenly, my foot tripped over something on the ground, and I almost fell. I screamed in horror and panic and looked at where my foot had stumbled; there was a lump on the floor, unidentifiable, next to the wall by one of the doors. I turned around to go back the way I came but heard a voice whispering:

"Rose?"

It was Ahmed's voice. I cried with joy. He was sitting on the floor, leaning against the wall, folding his legs into his body, crossing them with his forearms, and shaking his head up and down as if he had lost his mind. He was completely naked, and his clothes were scattered all over the floor. I approached him calmly and placed my hand on his head. He raised his head toward me and looked at me for a long time, scrutinizing my features as if he were unsure of who I was, and then asked me:

"Who am I, Rose?"

I panicked; I knew he was in an unnatural condition.

He was shivering from the cold. I wrapped my arms around him, and he leaned his head against my chest like a small child. Then he suddenly lifted his head and asked again:

"Who am I, Rose?"

I asked, "How can you know me but don't know yourself? You are Ahmed." He thought for a moment and replied:

"And who else?"

I was panicked; he scared me a lot. I shook him violently.

"What's wrong with you? What happened to you? Why are you naked like this? Why did you take off your clothes?"

He ignored what I said; he answered his question:

"I am my father, too. Did you know that?"

I didn't know how to respond. He simply looked at me and smiled:

I am also my grandfather. I am all of them. And they are all me. I was there. I reached there.

I told him to calm down and asked him to come home with me. I helped him to his feet, but then the camera fell from his lap, where he had been concealing it by wrapping his arms around it. It was buzzing like electricity. I bent down to pick it up. He screamed:

"NO, don't touch it."

But it was too late; I already held it in my hands. I immediately felt dizzy and was about to faint unless he quickly took it from me and threw it on the ground. He held me in his arms, covering me with his body as if he were trying to protect me from a particular danger.

"What happened?" I said, scared.

"Don't be afraid; I'm here with you. No harm will come to you as long as I'm with you."

"I'm still afraid. Let's get out of here."

His clothes were scattered on the ground. I picked them up, helped him put them on, and walked to the entrance of the alley, where patches of light appeared. It was the end of the night. We walked slowly until we reached the main street of the souq. He remained silent, hugging the camera, which continued to buzz occasionally.

At the entrance of the souq, horse carriages awaited early customers. One of the coachmen came over to help us get into the carriage, and then he drove us home.

All the way to the house, Ahmed remained silent, calm, and smiling, still clutching the camera and shivering from the cold. I held him in my arms. He rested his head on my chest like a little baby. Then, suddenly, he lifted his head and looked at my wrist.

"I'm sorry, Rose, the watch is gone."

"What watch?"

"It was a beautiful watch, with a red heart, a gift for you."

"Where did it go?"

"I put it on your wrist. I wanted it to be a surprise for you."

"What do you mean you put it on my wrist?"

He didn't answer and sank into deep thought.

"Do you mean someone attacked you and stole the watch?"

"No, no, I put it on your wrist." He paused in thought and continued in a low voice:

"Or maybe that's what I thought."

His words didn't make sense, so I didn't respond. I left him to himself, and he returned to his silence while hugging me tightly.

There was something different about him, something new; I didn't know how to describe it at the time. He combined multiple contradictions into one personality. He was calm yet boiling inside like a cauldron; silent, yet his eyes shone and spoke a language I didn't understand. He was physically exhausted, but sexually stimulated to the point of actively wooing me with his mouth and fingers. This behavior was unlike him; it felt strange and new, and he surprised me.

Usually, I was the one who teased him into giving me a kiss. I would snatch it from him, and he would blush as if I were the man and he were the woman. He wouldn't dare to go further with me out of shame or fear of hurting my feelings. But that night, he was lost in the moment, and his excitement grew to the point where I had to calm him down and ask him to wait until we got home, especially since the coachman was looking at us from time to time and sensed something was off.

As we arrived at my house, I gave the coachman Mariam's address along with a sum of money and asked him to deliver a message that Ahmed was okay and to reassure them that we were home.

We entered the apartment, and the first thing he did was wrap the camera in a cloth. Then he took off his clothes and sat on the bed. For the first time, he was naked with me in the apartment. He looked like he had just come out of a fight, with scratches and bruises covering most of his chest. I asked him, "Did you fight with someone?" He laughed and looked at me, wondering, "Why do you say that?" I pointed my finger at the bruises on his chest. He gazed at his reflection in the mirror, smiled enigmatically, and bathed. Despite the emotion and the strange ordeal he went through, he hid a secret joy, like a child returning from a trip to Wonderland. I could see him lost in thought, then he smiled as if he were reliving the events of his mysterious journey in his mind. After finishing in the bathroom, he came out and stood naked next to the bed. He looked at me as if he were seeing me for the first time. Then he approached me and took me in his arms; we had never made love before, and he had never tried it. There was a confidence and charm in his gaze that made me want to explode with desire. His touches radiated heat and passion that set my body ablaze, and his kisses sparked lust that traveled like electricity, awakening my desire. I didn't know how I ended up naked in his hands or how we got into bed together. He took me to a world of pleasure I had never known before, and I was tossed and turned in his hands as if I were unconscious, moving however he wanted and playing with my body while I surrendered to him completely. I was having my orgasm again and again and again and again, while he didn't ejaculate once. I was utterly exhausted. I didn't know how long we had been like this. I whispered to him to calm down, but he was too agitated to stop, and the sweat was pouring off him. He was pulling me towards him, squeezing me in his arms and pushing himself into me as if he wanted to melt me into him or melt into me. Finally, he ejaculated inside me like a volcano:

"No, no, he screamed, this is not supposed to happen."

I didn't understand what he meant. I thought he was apologizing to me.

"It's okay, I said. I wanted it to happen, too. I love you. It was great."

He leaned back, panting with exhaustion. But he never let go of me and did it again, just as hard, and when he ejaculated once more, he cried out in disappointment: "No, no, that's not supposed to happen."

His words worried me, so I asked him:

"Tell me, what's not okay?"

He looked at me and didn't answer. He wiped my body with a towel, dried off my sweat and his, then lay down next to me, kissed me, hugged me, and held me in his arms.

I was curious about what had happened and what had brought him to this state, so I waited until his breathing calmed down and he returned to normal. He stared at me as if seeing me for the first time. I looked into his eyes and asked him, "What happened there?"

He looked at me with a vague joy in his gaze, and then he smiled warmly that I didn't understand the reason for. He said with a tear in his eye:

"It was terrific, Rose. The world was here, pointing to his fist, in my hand, and the light was enormous, but it didn't hurt my eyes because I wasn't seeing with my eyes. I didn't need my body; I was disembodied, almost there, where no one else was. It was amazing, but suddenly..."

"Suddenly what?"

Ahmed didn't answer and remained silent, thinking.

"Suddenly what Ahmed? What happened?"

"Suddenly, the camera accidentally fell on the floor, and the flash accidentally went off and took her picture."

"Whose picture?"

"Rose."

"Rose? Me?"

"She's stuck there; She became a prisoner inside the camera."

"Who became a prisoner?"

"Rose."

"But I am here, Rose, in front of you."

He stared at me for a moment and then muttered, "Sure, sure." Then he got up to the camera, which was still humming intermittently.

"I have to release her."

He fiddled with the camera and tried to open it to no avail; he attempted to break it, but it didn't work. In despair, he took a box where I kept some valuables, emptied it, placed the camera inside, and locked it.

The following day, he emerged early with the box; that was the last time I saw the box and the camera until today.

In the days following that night, Ahmed was hesitant to work and didn't want to talk, especially about the incident, becoming angry if I mentioned it. He liked to hold me in his arms for hours; he didn't want to let me go. Sometimes he would leave the store for a long time, only to return looking sad. Afterward, he withdrew into himself and sank deeper into loneliness day after day until, one week after that night, he left and never came back, and no one heard anything about him.

François asked: "Why didn't you tell me the story of the camera before?"

I didn't tell anyone until today; I wanted to bury this story with me. But Mamdouh's arrival and the appearance of the camera were signals that I had to share what happened.

However, I said. "Ahmed has gone and taken the secret with him. We will never know what happened to him or his experience in that narrow alley in Bab Srijeh that night."

Chapter Eighteen

One day in Los Angeles, I met a psychiatrist of Arab descent who was attending a conference on hypnotism in psychology. He told me that he had presented a unique case at the conference where he was able to take a twenty-five-year-old patient's memory back to when she was six months old. During her hypnosis, she recalled things and events that her family and relatives could confirm.

He mentioned that efforts are underway to develop the technique of hypnotism so we can return the hypnotized person to their initial point of formation.

Is this possible? It cannot be confirmed for sure.

But what will the hypnotized person remember?

A more serious question is: "Is it possible to continue to what was before that moment? What would be there before that? Isn't it possible that our memory holds, for example, the history of our parents? Or perhaps even further back? Or maybe much further back than we think?

Rose wouldn't let me leave her side for the next two days, calling me into her room even though she was tired. She asked me about my father and mother and how they met, wanting to know everything, including how and where we lived. She inquired about every detail of our life in Beirut.

As for Louise, she spent her time swimming or going out with François to restaurants and clubs, and I sensed that she was delighted.

One morning, François came to tell me that Louise had left. I was very shocked; there was no explanation for her sudden departure. She didn't even say goodbye. However, she left a letter with François.

"Louise said You have to read it alone, away from everyone."

"Dear Mamdouh:

I'm sorry I left without saying goodbye; I thought it was for the best. I don't want to look into your eyes when I say goodbye, and I don't want to kiss you because I know I won't be able to hold back my tears. I don't want to cry anymore.

You're not mine; you're nobody's.

That's what I've realized since coming to France, and it's something I should have understood long ago. It's no secret that you're amazing in bed, but you struggle with belonging. You're unable to love, at least not enough to love me. I know you were trying;

I felt it, and I appreciate your effort, but I just couldn't take it anymore. Especially when I encountered your other side, François.

Pardon me for saying that François is the person I want; I loved him at first sight. He's the you I dream of and the you you can't be.

He has everything you lack; you are always distant, while he is always here. When I look at you, I feel lost; when I look at him, I feel safe.

I can only express at this moment that I hate both of you because I've lost you both. I wish I had known him before meeting you.

Don't hold a grudge against me, and kindly don't tell François why I left.

"Louise."

It is true that the letter was an honest expression of reality and that it relieved me of a heavy burden; however, it also frustrated me.

Isn't it enough that Lamees abandoned me? I felt a heavy weight, thinking I had become undesirable to women. I believed I had lost my charisma and attractiveness, leading to their abandonment. I won't pretend I was surprised by her departure; I sensed that something like this would happen soon. However, what surprised me was her connection to François, which didn't trouble me as much as it confused me. My relationship with François was still unclear and undefined, as it was still new.

François innocently asked me why Louise had left and, with his usual kindness, inquired if something had happened between us or if something had upset her. He had no clue at all, especially when he said.

"She invited me to visit her in California and insisted a lot that I should do.

I smiled, "California is beautiful and worth a visit."

"Maybe you and I could go together."

"I will never go back there, my place is in Syria, I think you should go alone, you will like America."

"Do you think so?"

"Yes, especially since Louise will be your guide there."

François smiled slyly and then burst out laughing.

Everything feels normal for François, and nothing seems worth taking seriously or tragically. I admire the simplicity with which he approaches life. Perhaps that's what Louise meant and what she desired.

In such situations, one reviews their behavior and actions and puts them under analysis, a process of self-criticism. I asked myself, "Am I that bad without knowing it?" I must have complicated Louise's life and made her miserable. Couldn't I have taken life as easily as François? I wonder if that's what Louise was looking for, too?

All these questions made me realize that François's appearance in my life would change it significantly.

We stayed in Nice for several days, during that time I kept in touch with my sister in Damascus, updating her about Rose and François. It was surprising yet happy news for her and Zeina.

But there was another reason I called Hanan: I asked her to contact the mukhtar and request Lamees's number in France.

Louise's departure was an opportunity. I believe the fates are playing an essential role in a strange game here, and I have an odd feeling that they are guiding me in a specific direction. Isn't it weird that Louise is leaving while Lamees is in France at the same time I am? Isn't that a sign I should make a move and take advantage of this opportunity? Isn't that a sign that I should help the fates and nudge them toward arranging our meeting? The idea of Lamees being in France excites and frightens me at the same time. It excites me because of the possibilities. It scares me that if I push things too far, I could lose her forever.

Hanan was able to obtain the number from the mukhtar. It was now my responsibility to bring Lamees back and mend the relationship with her. I had to be more careful in my interactions with her.

I called her at the number. A man's voice spoke to me in French: "Hello, who is it?"

I felt disappointed. It was the voice of a man who had just awakened from sleep.

"Is Lamees there?"

His voice faded momentarily, and then I heard Lamees's voice.

"Hello"

My heart raced as I listened to her. I said hesitantly, "Hello, Lamees." She immediately recognized my voice and shouted with joy, "Mamdouh? What a surprise, where are you?"

"How are you?"

"Very well. And you?"

"I'm fine."

"No, you're not fine; you look sad. Where are you?"

"Who is this man with you?"

"Never mind him."

"Who is he?"

"I barely know him, so never mind him. You tell me, are you still in France?"

"Yes, I am."

"Do you need me? If you need me, I can come to you now."

"Where are you?"

"I'm in Paris; I've been at the conference since we arrived, and it's almost over. Today is the last day, and after that, I'm free to be with you if you want me."

Indeed, fate is arranging things for me.

I asked her, "How is Isabelle?"

She laughed and said in a reproachful voice, filled with humor and excitement, "Do you want Isabelle?"

"No," I growled, "not at all."

"Well, she's gone on her own. She went to Lyon. Are you still angry with her and me?"

I didn't answer. She was silent for a while and then asked in a serious voice, "Who was that girl with you at the airport?"

"You mean Louise? She's an American friend."

"She seems to be more than a friend."

"She's not anymore, she dumped me."

Lamees burst out laughing.

"What are you laughing at?"

"You're in a bad situation. I didn't expect you to stoop so low."

"It's your fault. You know"

"Me?"

"Louise has discovered that I'm distracted by someone else."

"And I'm the one on your mind?"

"You've become the main thing in my life."

"Listen, tell me where you are and I'll come and ask for your forgiveness."

"I'm in Nice, and you're still not taking things seriously. "

"You never know how much I love you."

"I no longer understand you."

"Tell me, how is Nice?"

"The weather is great."

Lamees exclaimed with delight. "That's great! Can we go swimming?"

The fates were doing more for me than I had anticipated.

"Of course we can."

"Then I'll take the night train and we'll be at the beach in the morning. What do you think?"

My heart skipped a beat; this was more than I expected. I was so happy, but something inside me warned against giving in to the joy, keeping me alert and ready for some of her diabolical tricks. Yet, another concern nagged at me—something I hadn't considered before: François.

What if she falls in love with him too? He has become my rival, and he is a rival to be reckoned with. He emerged from the past to unwittingly capture Louise's heart.

I told François about Lamees coming to spend a few days with us. He laughed and said:

"And who is this Lamees, too? You surprise me. Can't you stay without women for a day?"

"But Lamees means a lot to me. I said this sentence spontaneously, but François looked at me and laughed."

"Are you warning me not to go near her?"

I told him I would meet her at the train station and spend the day together in the city, walking around and sightseeing. François insisted on taking me to the station to meet her and invite her to the villa, where he would introduce her to Rose. Then we would have breakfast together before going our separate ways. Alarm bells rang in my head. Fear began to creep in.

We arrived at the station well ahead of time that morning at my insistence. François had jokingly dressed in clothes similar to mine, styled his hair the same way I did, and held up a bouquet of nearly identical flowers. He said joyfully and excitedly:

"We will intrigue her."

He had no idea how much anxiety he caused me or the fear I felt standing next to him, as if I were on the edge of a difficult exam. When the train stopped, he said that standing next to each other would be much more fun to shock her. The passengers started to disembark. The station wasn't crowded, but a few passengers got off, mostly students and a few women. My eyes wandered among the passengers in all the carriages, checking them one by one, but I didn't see her. I felt anxious and upset. I feared it was a prank. But François tugged on my hand as he looked at a girl in jeans, covering her hair with a French hat like a teenage boy. She was standing at a distance from us with her bag, looking at us quietly and smiling. I scrutinized her features, and it was her, Lamees, the one with the surprises.

"That's her," I said as I grabbed François.

We walked towards her at a brisk pace, François deliberately annoying me and walking right next to me. When we got close to her, her smile disappeared as she looked at us in surprise, but she didn't hesitate for long as she threw herself into my arms, gave me a long hug, and kissed me intimately.

How I love this Lamees, despite all her contradictions, she reveals her love to me freely and spontaneously:

I loved her more and more, and I was grateful to her for not letting me down in front of François. She suddenly turned away, staring at François in astonishment and then looking back at me in wonder.

"This is François, my brother."

She held out her hand, and François took it and kissed it.

I asked her, "How did you recognize me from him?"

She laughed: "Your looks exposed you."

"How so?"

"There's a fear in them, just like yours that night."

François said: "How beautiful you are, ma'am, I didn't expect that."

"Where did you get this cute brother?" she asked in amazement.

"It's a long story; I'll tell you later."

"No, I will tell it to you on the way to the villa," François said as he led her to the car.

He looked at me and said, laughing loudly, "It looks like we are going to compete for the heart of this beautiful belle."

Lamees laughed; she liked his comment, but I didn't like it at all. I regretted bringing her, especially as I watched him grab her hand as they walked to the car, laughing and whispering while I trailed behind, dragging her bag. She got into the car's front seat next to him, and I sat alone in the back seat, like discarded garbage.

I felt as though I had just given her another weapon to continue her revenge against me while I struggled to reach a truce with her.

As François shared our story, she listened intently and quietly. While I relaxed in my seat, gazing at the sea, I felt sullen and in a bad mood. Louise's abandonment had taken a toll on me and shaken my self-confidence.

We arrived at the villa, and while I felt nervous, I did my best to appear cheerful and calm. François asked me to show Lamees around the villa and the garden while he informed Rose of our arrival and prepared breakfast.

We walked through the garden, where Lamees admired the view and the beautiful landscape surrounding the villa. Suddenly, she turned around and said:

"What do you think of my outfit?"

"It's beautiful. You look special and different, like a teenager. You are always beautiful."

"Does it remind you of anything? I wore these clothes just for you."

"Does it have to remind me of something?"

"Doesn't it remind you of Lamees in college? It reminds me of you anyway. That was my way of dressing when we were together. After you called me, I suddenly felt strange in my clothes. I wanted to bring back the Lamees you knew and loved. I wanted to appeal to you. Didn't you say you miss Lamees?"

You know I love you no matter who you are, but what happened at your home and on the plane still confuses me and makes me wonder about who you really are.

She took my hand and led me to a distant corner of the garden, then drew me closer and gave me a long kiss, which restored sunshine and joy to my soul.

But she didn't stop at the kiss; she began pressing her body against mine. she said in a frantic, insistent voice:

"I missed you; I can't wait any longer. I want you now."

"I want you even more."

"I wish we had gone to a hotel first."

"I wanted that too, but I was afraid and hesitant. I can't predict your reactions anymore. I fear I might misbehave and hurt your feelings. I try to please you, but you ...."

"Don't continue," she said, touching my mouth. "Don't continue, please, don't waste the magic of this moment on questions. Tell me, are you pleased now?"

"I'm delighted. I can't believe you're with me."

"Then don't let any other thoughts spoil the moment. I am now with you and in your arms, I want you to unleash your emotions and love me as you have never loved anyone before."

"I have never loved anyone else."

"Think of us as two people who have just met and are on the cusp of a big new love story. Forget Mamdouh and Lamees, their shadow is heavy."

We heard François' voice looking for us. We interrupted our conversation and went towards him.

"Come on, Rose is waiting for you. She'll meet you in her room."

Rose lay in her bed, a quiet smile on her face, when we entered. Upon seeing Lamees, her eyes lit up and she beamed at her with a wide grin, gazing at her face.

"Come closer to me, Rose said to Lamees, sit next to me, look at me."

Lamees looked at her and blushed.

"How beautiful you are! Once I was as beautiful as you are, as radiant as you are."

"You are still beautiful."

"Enjoy your beauty. It is a gift to be cherished and enjoyed."

"And you?" said Lamees, "Have you enjoyed your beauty and youth?"

Rose looked at Lamees, trying to figure out where she was going with this question, then smiled and said:

"I loved once. And that's enough for me."

Lamees's face fell, her smile disappeared, and her eyes filled with tears. She rushed out of the room.

Rose turned to me and whispered, "I see love in her eyes. Go and wipe her tears." I must have said something inappropriate.

I left the room searching for Lamees, reflecting on Rose's words. She stood near the raspberry tree in the garden, gazing at the distant sea. I approached her quietly, and when she sensed my presence, she said, pointing to a branch:

"Look at that worm on the branch."

"What's wrong with it?"

"Poor thing, I pity it."

"Why?"

"It's only a matter of days, and it will be trapped inside its cocoon."

"But then it will emerge as a beautiful butterfly flying through the gardens from flower to flower."

Lamees fell silent as she watched the worm with compassion and whispered sadly:

"I can't imagine being inside the cocoon; I could die. I wonder how it spends its time in there. I wonder if it's in pain. Doesn't it miss the light?"

"This is part of its life cycle, and I believe it enjoys its imprisonment just as much as it enjoys its flight. I feel that each stage has its charm."

"But what if it can't get out?"

"What do you mean?"

"What if it tries to get out but can't and is still trapped?"

She started crying profusely while I wiped her tears with my fingers.

We heard François's voice calling us to breakfast.

At the table, François dominated the conversation while Lamees remained silent and distant.

"What's wrong, Ms. Lamees? You don't seem to be feeling well?"

"I'm sorry, but I'm tired from traveling."

I joked: "A thick worm on your raspberry tree is bothering her."

Lamees laughed and said:

"No, it's a gentle worm, it didn't bother me, on the contrary, I liked it, and I think at one point it stopped and raised its head towards me, it must have said hello to me."

We laughed, and Lamees's face brightened up again,

"Take me to the beach, I want to swim."

I asked François: Can we go swimming?

"Sure, you can change your clothes here, and here are my car keys, you can drive her around the city."

Lamees entered the room and came out wearing a thin dress over her swimsuit. It was unbuttoned in the front. She sat beside me. She deliberately let the dress fall to the sides, dramatically accentuating her legs. She rested her head on my shoulder. I was in an unenviable position. I just wanted to throw myself on top of her. I put my hand on her knee and she didn't mind. She said, "Find us a quiet place."

We went to the beach. Lamees picked an empty spot away from everyone. She removed her dress and waded into the water while I followed her. The water was cold, and the sea was rough, but Lamees insisted on staying in. It was nice; the cold water and the movement of the waves lifted her spirits and made her feel playful laughter. We played like kids, and the pretenses disappeared. She threw herself into my arms like she used to do in college, and I was so happy, I felt like I had finally achieved what I wanted. I thought I was in paradise. After Lamees had had enough of swimming, she got out of the water and said, shivering from the cold, "Let's have coffee and listen to music." We went to one of the bars on the beach; she sat in her chair and leaned her head back. I liked to watch her, and I knew she liked that I watched her. Her dress was unbuttoned primarily, revealing her breasts and legs in a sexy way. She sat glued to me, resting her shoulder on my head, swaying to the music with her eyes closed. I couldn't control myself anymore, I reached up to her knee and she closed her eyes and whispered: "I want to hold you, I want you to take me in your arms, let's dance." The cafe was empty; we were the only ones on the dance floor. She was swaying with her eyes closed, pressing her body against mine, pressing her fingers against my ass, and then she started running her hot breath down my neck. I savor the dry salt on her lips.

She whispered warmly, "The smell of the sea on your neck turns me on. I want to be alone with you now. I can't take it anymore."

"We can go back to the villa if you want."

"Are we going to be comfortable there?"

"Of course, we have our private room."

Her behavior was unfamiliar to me. She's definitely not the shy Lamees I knew, but I wasn't complaining; she's even more captivating and alluring.

On the way back in the car, she rested her head and closed her eyes, letting the air play with her hair. Then she grabbed my hand and kissed it hungrily, sucking on my fingers one by one.

I said, "I have become more and more fond of you than ever before."

"No one could turn me on like you did, she said, shoving my hand between her thighs. No one could understand my body language like you did. What have you done to me? Nothing satisfies me anymore."

"All I did was love you."

She remained silent and rested her head on my shoulder, allowing my hand to revel in its warm prison. Then she suddenly said:

"How marvelous Rose is. How touching her love story is. Then she turned to me, gave me a serious look, and said:

"I will never be like Rose."

She continued, fearful: "I can't be like her; her story makes me sick. I pity her and sympathize with her at the same time. But I can't be like her."

After a while, she looked at me and asked, "Do you think I can be like her? Do you think I can love like her? No, I don't think I can."

"But you love me, don't you?"

I looked at her, searching her eyes for the answer to my question, but all I could see was fear in her gaze. I stayed silent. When we arrived at the villa, I was eager to head straight to the room. But François met us as soon as we arrived: "Rose wants to see you."

Rose was in bed, as usual, holding her golden eagle tie. She looked at me and pleaded, "Can you take me to visit Ahmed?"

"To Syria?"

"Yes, I feel that my end is near. I don't want to die far away from him."

Lamees was standing next to me, listening to Rose's words:

"I have a strong feeling that heaven has sent you to fulfill a wish that was impossible till now; to die near Ahmed."

"Damn it, Lamees said in an angry voice, then burst into tears and rushed out of the room, chanting, "Damn it, damn it, damn it," she was so angry.

"Forgive her, she's compassionate and doesn't like the idea of death," I said to Rose:

"It's okay, I understand her very well."

Neither François nor I could refuse Rose's request, even though her health couldn't handle the strain of traveling.

In the end, we all agreed to travel to Damascus.

In the evening, Lamees called her father to let him know where she was in Nice. She told him that she was staying with me at Rose's villa and also mentioned that we were all headed to Damascus.

My promised night with Lamees didn't come true. It seems I misunderstood the game of fate that led to our meeting. I didn't know what went wrong. I couldn't get close to her that night or the nights that followed; her mood had changed completely. She couldn't stand talking to me, and she spent the rest of our time in Nice on the terrace, watching the sea and the sky or walking in the nearby forest. François and I tried unsuccessfully to bring a smile back to her face.

Chapter Nineteen

If pain is the body's alarm signal that something is wrong, and if hunger is the body's way of telling us it needs food, what does the body demand from the urgency of lust? What need or defect does it seek to alert us about?

At the airport, Abu Hamza greeted us and kissed me warmly. He was astonished when he met François and nearly mistook me for him. In the car, Lamees sat beside her father while I was behind her with Rose and François, watching her hair blow in the breeze and feeling frustrated.

The mukhtar sensed something was wrong as he looked at Lamees, pale and silent. He then gave me a questioning look in the mirror. I avoided his gaze and his silent inquiries, hoping that things between Lamees and me would return to normal.

As for Rose, she was quiet too, gazing intently out the car window at the people and traffic on the streets, her eyes functioning like a journalist's camera, capturing and storing everything. She muttered softly to herself:

"Everything has changed; I don't recognize anything."

She appeared to be interested in the entrance to the city, in the Eastern Gate area called Bab Sharqui. She said, looking around everywhere:

We're close to Bab Touma, right? I know this area; it hasn't changed much. Take me there.

"I think you should rest first and then return for a tour."

"No, I can't wait, take me now."

The car entered the Bab Touma area. I started to mention the names of some places and landmarks, and she enthusiastically supported my words. As we drove through the narrow streets, her face lit up, and she said, "This place hasn't changed much, my God, it's like I was here yesterday." She asked the mukhtar to slow down a bit in some spots, explaining to François like a tour guide. When we arrived at the French hospital, she exclaimed happily, "This is the hospital, isn't it? This is the hospital, isn't it?"

"Take me to the Abu Rummana neighborhood. I want to check out my apartment and what's left of Rose's salon."

"Abu Rummana has changed a lot."

"It doesn't matter, I want to see it."

Then she smiled: "We're going next to the Barada River, right?"

Her smile vanished as we passed by the riverbank. "This is where I used to walk a lot when bored. I used to come here and watch the water flow," she told François. "Oh my God, where is the water? The Barada is dying, just like me, can I stand on its bank for a bit?"

Rose asked to leave the car, but she couldn't stand it for long and kept repeating her phrase: "Everything has changed."

We continued to Umayyad Square. As the car drove toward the Malki area and Abu Rummaneh, she seemed very focused, frequently asking us to slow down or stop and then turning around to look at the buildings and side streets.

She said sadly, "The buildings are many and the streets are new; they weren't here before; they were all orchards."

At one corner, she screamed:

"Stop, it's here, here it is." She pointed her finger towards a tall building, and it was behind this building. Yes, I remember that exactly.

But behind the building, there was another modern structure with several floors. She hesitated moment, then said, "Yes, unfortunately, the salon was located here, in this new building. What a shame."

"Can I step down for a while?"

She paused at the entrance of the building, turning around to survey its surroundings, and then exclaimed excitedly:

"Yes, it's the same building, but it's been remodeled a lot."

Rose came back to life. Her voice came alive as she said, "Yes, here was Rose's salon in this ground-floor apartment, which has been turned into an apartment, and look, François, my apartment was here on the second floor, right above the salon."

She explained to him how she would walk south toward Barada, east toward the Abu Rummana neighborhood, or north toward the Muhajireen area.

"That's enough for today, Rose. Let's go to the hotel. I think you should rest now," I said

"No, I have to go first to visit Ahmed. I want to put flowers on his grave."

Of course, we couldn't convince her to postpone it. We went to the cemetery. Along the way, she asked what the area was called and how far it was from the city center.

The sun was just about to set when Rose stood at my father's grave, sat on the edge, placed the bouquet, and remained silent as we walked around. Lamees stayed outside the cemetery fence, watching from a distance with her father, who insisted on staying to take us back to the hotel.

Rose asked me, "Read what is written on the tombstone." I read his name and the date of his death. She gently ran her hand over the grave, feeling it tenderly, and then asked to be left alone. We stepped outside the fence, leaving her by herself. When I returned to her a little later, she was softly singing in a whisper:

"When he holds me in his arms and whispers sweet words of love, life becomes rosy."

The mukhtar dropped us off at the hotel, and then he and Lamees left. She was undoubtedly lost in a sea of thoughts, and I wished she would open up and share what was on her mind. But she was impossible with everyone, including her father.

Rose went to bed immediately, while François insisted on accompanying me to visit Hanan and Zeina.

It was a touching and hilarious meeting. François was so excited as he hugged Hanan and Zeina, constantly repeating, "You're my sister? You're my sister? Unbelievable, and I'm the uncle of this beautiful girl?" We stayed up late discussing various topics, with numerous photos displayed around the salon and all the albums open. We lingered that way until almost morning. I dropped him off at the hotel and then headed back to my apartment.

I was tired and had been without sleep for about twenty-four hours. Exhausted, I lay on my bed and closed my eyes when I heard a soft knock on the door. I opened the door, and it was Lamees.

"Can I come in?" she said shyly. Her face was pale, I said:

"Of course, are you okay?"

"No, I'm not, that's why I want to be near you. I feel scared, and I feel like I need you."

She moved closer and hugged me, then began to cry.

"I thought you were mad at me, you were outraged," I said

"Was it showing?"

"You didn't speak to me for two days or even look at me."

"Maybe I was angry, but not at you."

"Who, then?"

She didn't answer; she went into the bedroom.

"I love this room, we have so many memories here."

She undressed until she was almost naked, then turned off the light and slipped into bed.

"I want to fall asleep on your chest tonight; I haven't slept well for days."

I couldn't believe it, I took off all my clothes and threw myself on the bed next to her. She pushed her soft body against me, wrapped her arm around me, her leg around my leg, and lay her head on my chest until we were like one body. I ran my fingers through her hair, kissed her forehead, and tried to caress her, but she yawned and whispered with closed eyes: "Stop, don't do anything, please, let's sleep today, I'm so tired and so are you."

"How can I sleep with your breasts caressing my chest?"

She kissed me, laughing, and said: "Whoever is patient gets what he wants." Despite my fatigue, I found it difficult to sleep, feeling the warmth of her body pressed against mine. She slept like a baby.

I woke up to the sound of the phone. I opened my eyes and looked beside me to make sure Lamees was there. She was indeed right there, sound asleep. The caller was the mukhtar. I felt confused and stammered, afraid that he would come to visit and find Lamees in my bed. But he just wanted to check on me. I knew he wanted to see me to ask about the nature of my relationship with Lamees. I told him I wanted to see Abu Jassim to check on him and take the photo to show Rose. He offered to come and pick me up, but I preferred to meet at Abu Jassim's place.

I stood beside the bed, looking at the naked Lamees in my bed. I kissed her, covered her up, got dressed, and went to Abu Jassim's house.

Chapter Twenty

Abu Jassim was excitedly waiting for us, as he had been keeping track of my travel news from the mukhtar. He was still in the same condition. He could only see two eyes fixed on him, watching and staring at him constantly.

I asked about Abu Anwar. The mukhtar said he was still in the hospital and that his condition was getting worse. The doctors mentioned that he was experiencing a mental breakdown and had not yet found the cause.

I asked Abu Jassim for the photo, and he reluctantly handed it over. I examined the image, noticing that the woman's face had become so distinct it almost overshadowed everything else. The watch on her wrist was still ticking. I recalled the story of the watch that Rose had mentioned in her tale about my father's bizarre experience. I studied it closely, wondering if it was the same watch. The image of the red heart on its dial was clearly visible. The mukhtar took it, gazed at her, then turned to look at me:

"Every time I look at her, my skin crawls."

"Why?"

"Her look is strange."

"In what way?"

"There's life in it, sometimes I think she's blinking."

"I'll take it to show it to Rose."

I put the picture in an envelope, said goodbye to the mukhtar, and headed to the hotel. There, I was welcomed by François, who had just woken up.

"Come look at Rose, she's been on the balcony since morning."

Hanan and Zeina were in Rose's room with her. They were all on the balcony overlooking the Barada, and Rose listened to them and laughed before returning to contemplate the river. She smiled when she saw me.

Your sister is wonderful, and so is Zeina. You all remind me of Ahmed. Thank you, Mamdouh.

"What for?" I said, wondering

"Because you appeared out of nowhere and brought me to where I should be and belong."

I said, laughing:

"Guess what we're having for breakfast today?"

She thought for a while, but then I continued: "You're not going to guess, we'll have foul and hummus for breakfast today. Did you eat that in Ahmed's day?" Rose laughed and said, "That was your father's favorite food."

After breakfast at the hotel restaurant, Hanan and Zeina left us. We returned to the room, but Rose could hardly move; yet, she refused any assistance while walking. At times, she leaned on François to navigate the stairs.

Rose went straight back to the balcony and sat, watching the river. I told her that the picture in the camera was with me, which piqued her interest. She straightened up, asking to see it. I handed the envelope to François; he opened it, took out the photo, looked at it, opened his mouth, and said, "Amazing. Unbelievable." Rose eagerly grabbed the picture from his hand and took a closer look, then said in a whispered voice as if enchanted, "Oh my God, it's really moving."

Rose continued: "She has my watch on her wrist."

"Your watch?"

"Yes, it is the exact watch described by Ahmed, with a red heart on the dial."

François remarked, "Unbelievable, it must be an illusion."

I asked Rose: "Did you recognize the woman?"

Rose laughed and said as she looked at the photo: "Of course I recognize her."

"Really, Oh my God, who is she?"

Rose asked François to take a photo out of one of the pockets of her bag. He rummaged through the bag and pulled a photo of a beautiful girl. He looked at it and smiled, "Really, how did I not notice that?"

He gave me the photo, and I compared the two images, and the resemblance was unmistakable.

"So, who is this girl?"

"It's me."

"What?"

"Yes, this is a picture of me when I was twenty. Look how much she looks like the photo girl."

"That's weird."

"And this watch," Rose said. "It's mine, the gift I didn't get."

She turned to me and said, "Leave the photo with me. I need it for something." Then she put it back in the envelope.

"Now let me rest."

François had a date with Hanan and Zeina. They had agreed to tour old Damascus to show him its landmarks. François was very happy talking about his sister in front of Rose, repeating the word "sister" as if he were learning it all over again. Rose was delighted.

The photo captured my imagination. What troubled me most was that every time a piece of the puzzle became clear, it grew more mysterious.

I returned to the apartment; Lamees had left me a note with a heart and the words "thank you" inside, signed with a kiss at the bottom.

Chapter Twenty-One

No matter how much time passes and how old I get, I will always see myself as a child. That's how I view Lamees too. Sometimes, when I close my eyes, I see that college girl, her shadow wandering toward me at the university, her hair blowing in the sunlight. She smiles and says to me, "Hi, I'm Lamees." There will always be a special corner in my memory for this scene, repeated over and over again. Every time Lamees reaches out her hand to me, smiling and saying, "Hi, I'm Lamees," my heart beats with joy.

The phone rang while I was asleep; it was after midnight. François's voice on the other end said, "Come quickly, Mamdouh, Rose has disappeared!"

I rushed to the hotel; François awaited me at the entrance. He said he had left Hanan and Zeina and returned at midnight to find her bed empty. The hotel clerk mentioned that she had ordered a taxi to take her to the Bab Srijeh neighborhood.

We took a taxi that drove us to Bab Srijeh. The neighborhood was dark, with only a few lights in different corners. The long souq was empty. François and I stood at its entrance, feeling confused.

"Where could she have gone?" François asked me.

I might know; I once came here with my father before he passed away. He went to a specific place, and perhaps she was there.

We arrived at the narrow sub-alley where my father once stood at the corner in fear. I hesitated; I, too, felt a kind of fear. I remembered the dark alley from the dream.

François glanced at me and noticed my hesitation. "Is there something wrong?"

I said, "Nothing, let's go into the alley."

The alley was narrow and very dark, so we walked carefully. It wound around, and at one of the turns, François found an envelope on the ground. It was the same envelope that had held the photo, but it was empty.

"She was here," François said,

We walked to the end of the lane, which led us to another lane and then to the main street, where there were lights, people, and cars. There was no sign of Rose. François exclaimed in horror:

"Oh my God, I'm afraid something has happened to her."

"If she came out of this street, she might have gotten into a car and returned to the hotel."

We called the hotel, and they said she hadn't returned. François implored me:

"Could she have gone to visit his grave?"

There was no other option. We took a car and drove to the cemetery.

There we found her.

She sat still on the edge of the grave, frozen in place. We rushed to her side. She was wearing a coat and shivering from the cold, but when she saw us, she smiled. And she said, "I'm okay, don't worry. I'm sorry if I scared you, but I had something to take care of by myself."

As we drove back in the car, Rose was breathing heavily. François was holding her close to his chest when she whispered to him, smiling:

"I'm relieved for you now; you have a family. I was always afraid that I would die and leave you alone."

François replied, smiling awkwardly, "I have never been lonely with you by my side."

She turned to me, extended her hand, and said, "Thank you again, we both finally found what we were looking for."

"Take care of François."

Those were Rose's last words.

Rose died in François's arms, smiling, her hand in her coat pocket clutching a tie that featured a golden eagle.

Rose and her eagle finally flew away.

We rushed to the French hospital, where she was officially pronounced dead. François was in shock. He said:

"The doctors had been telling me for a while that her days were numbered, but I didn't expect it to happen so quickly."

Hanan and Zeina arrived quickly and were heartbroken by the news. Zeina cried heavily while François remained stoic and calm. He stood beside Rose's bed, holding her hand, unwilling to let them cover her face. I took care of all the necessary paperwork and formalities.

Now, Rose was prepared for burial.

I asked François, "What do you want to do? Do you want to take her back to France to be buried there? I can make all the arrangements."

But François said, looking at her lying in bed:

"Can we bury her next to Ahmed, where she belongs, as she wished?

"I will see what I can do."

I called the mukhtar and told him what had happened. He was, of course, surprised and quickly came to the hospital. I informed him about François's wishes. The mukhtar was more knowledgeable than I was; he told me to leave it to him.

Then Lamees came.

I had never seen her so angry; her face was pale, yellowish, and sparks flew from her eyes. When I approached her, she pushed me away.

The enigmatic Lamees has returned.

I had to endure the persona she adopted whenever we were in Rose's presence or she was mentioned. I didn't attempt to ask her anything; she was in no state to be approached. I kept my distance and observed her from afar. But I wondered to myself: "What is my fault? Why is she so angry with me? I knew she loved me; she loved me very much, so I couldn't find an answer to my questions.

At noon, I asked François to go to the hotel and get some sleep, but he refused to release Rose's hand.

"I can't sleep alone in the hotel"

"You won't go to the hotel, Hanan said, you'll go home with us to my house, your sister's house," she said, holding his hand in hers.

He looked at her quizzically: "Can I really do that?"

"Of course you can, you are my brother. We are family."

François released Rose's hand, took one last look at her, kissed her, covered her face, and left holding Hanan's hand.

I went out to look for Lamees.

Chapter Twenty-Two

Most physical ailments are psychological in origin, say advocates of psychiatry. We carry our illnesses and sicknesses with us and keep them inside. However, we also carry medicine.. These illnesses may find some relief through laboratory medicine, but the real medicine lies within us. All we have to do is seek it within ourselves.

In the evening, the mukhtar called to inform me that Rose could be buried in the same cemetery, in accordance with Islamic laws and rituals. I asked him about Lamees, and he said she hadn't been feeling well since returning from France. He mentioned that he had tried to ask her about the cause of her depression, but he was unsuccessful and didn't receive any response from her.

"Rose's death has affected her a lot...give her time, she'll be back to normal."

"I wonder if that's really the reason."

I understood what he meant but feigned ignorance and asked, "Could there be another reason?

"I began to wonder why she was depressed whenever you were around."

I laughed and said, "Do you think it's because I'm around her that she's depressed?"

"Don't take things lightly. I really want to understand what's going on between you two."

"Believe me, I want to understand as much as you do. Anyway, let's finish burying Rose; maybe things will calm down."

She wasn't anywhere I knew. She didn't answer her phone. I went to her apartment, but no one replied. Just before midnight, the doorbell rang. I opened it, and it was the mukhtar:

"Is Lamees okay?" I said worriedly

"It's not Lamees, it's Abu Jassim."

There was an unexpected surprise.

"What happened? You had me worried."

"You won't believe your eyes, look who's here?"

It was Abu Jassim.

He stood in the darkness, far from the doorstep, wearing dark glasses. He lifted them with a big smile and rushed towards me, hugging and kissing me in the midst of my surprise and astonishment.

"What? You are seeing, Abu Jassim?"

"It's a miracle."

"How did it happen? I said emotionally. Come on in. and tell me"

Abu Jassim and the mukhtar came in. I was stunned with surprise.

"It's a dream, a strange dream. Last night, a girl came to me in the dream, grabbed my hand, and said: "Look at me." I told her I couldn't because I'm blind. She replied that if I tried to look at her, I would see her. I held her face in my hand and began to feel its contours with my fingers. Her silhouette started to appear before me, and then the spectrum gradually became clearer and clearer until her features were completely distinct. She smiled at me and then disappeared. In the morning, I opened my eyes to find that I could see. "

"This is really strange; it's truly a miracle."

"I don't know what happened, but I know it had something to do with the photo."

"How so?"

"I think the girl who came to me in the dream might be the same as the one in the photo. I'm not quite sure, so I want to see the photo. I want to see the face of the girl you said was in the picture. Can I see her now? I want to see the one who caused all of this."

"Unfortunately, the photo is missing. Rose took it with the envelope, and when we found the envelope, the picture wasn't there."

When I met François the next day, I asked him about the photo, but he had no idea.

We all went to the hospital, where we transported Rose in her coffin to the cemetery to conclude a strange and mysterious love story between Rose and Ahmed.

I can't tell if it was a sad or happy ending.

François looked relieved to see the two graves next to each other.

Lamees was not there. She didn't attend the burial ceremony.

"I think Rose died happy," François told me. "This ending was better than I expected for her."

On our way back after the burial, the mukhtar gave him a bag, which he said the hospital had given him. It contained Rose's clothes and belongings that she had carried with her when she was hospitalized.

At home, we opened the bag. Among the items were her coat and handbag. Inside the bag were money, various items, and a watch.

I was shocked when I saw the watch. I shouted:

"It's the same. There's a red heart inside the dial; it's the same wristwatch as the one in the photo. The hospital officials stated they had removed it from her wrist."

"Strange, where did Rose get it from?" François wondered.

There was nothing special among the rest of the items.

But when François rummaged through the coat pockets, he found the photo. I took it quickly

"It's the same photo. But ...."

"But what?"

"She's gone, disappeared."

"Who disappeared?"

"The girl, the one with the watch and the weird look."

We took the photo and checked it. There was no girl; she had vanished from the picture. Only Abu

Jassim and Abu Anwar were present. There was no trace of the girl in the image; the only memory of her was the watch we found, which was still working.

Something must have happened. The girl can't just appear in the photo and then disappear for no reason. How did the watch end up back with Rose? How did it get out of the photo and onto Rose's wrist? Something must have occurred to Rose in that alley in Bab Srijeh.

"Something Like what?" François asked

I don't know, but when I think about what happened with my father and what Rose said about him mentioning that the girl was a prisoner in the picture, it seems clear now that she has been freed, released from her prison. Strangely enough, this coincides with Abu Jassim's sight. Isn't that strange?

"But who is she?"

"I don't know, the answer lies there.

"Where?" François asked

In that narrow alley where my father stood one day, where Rose found Ahmed lying naked, and where we found the envelope Rose was carrying. The secret is there, and so is the answer."

"But we went in it together; we found nothing."

"You're right. However, if there was any secret or mystery, it is now buried with Ahmed and Rose. "

The story concluded with the deaths of the people involved.

No matter how much we discussed and analyzed its details since discovering the box, we couldn't reach any answers.

That night, François gave me the watch and asked me to keep it. He said Rose would've been more than happy if I kept it and gave it to someone dear to me.

Chapter Twenty-Three

Am I talking too much about sex? Maybe I don't know why; perhaps I'm searching for answers. Regardless, I find myself compelled to write about it. I love how it captivates and controls me; I can't resist it. I always feel that sex gives me an impulse that directs my actions and shapes my way of thinking.

As for Lamees, I don't know; I sometimes wonder what force is driving me towards her, and I ask myself a lot: "What do I want from her, love or sex?"

But it doesn't matter anymore.

No matter how much I try in vain to cling to the wall,

I am sliding toward my inevitable abyss,

toward my destiny,

toward Lamees.

The next morning, we all went to the cemetery and placed myrtle branches and bouquets on Rose and Ahmed's graves. Lamees didn't show up and remained invisible with her phone off.

On the third day, she arrived. She approached the cemetery dressed in black, with a black shawl covering her hair and wearing dark glasses. She didn't come any closer; she stayed back, and I continued watching her from a distance.

Lamees turned me on just by looking at her in whatever outfit she wore. I waited for the entire family to leave and then approached her cautiously. She took off her glasses and gazed at me for a long time. I stayed silent, waiting for her reaction. She came closer and kissed me on the cheek, saying in a voice that had a lot of coquetry in it:

"Do you accept this as an apology?"

I was weak for Lamees; one word from her, and I would drop at her feet.

"Why are you angry with me?"

"Let's go to a quiet place where we can talk freely."

We drove her car to a café in Dummar; it was beautiful and overlooked Damascus.

"You have a lot of anger towards me."

"You know very well that's not true. I'm just angry at myself and scared."

"Of what?"

"It's Rose. I see myself in her, and it scares me."

"What exactly are you afraid of?"

"I'm afraid to return to being alone; it scares me. I've lived through it before, and I barely made it. When I ventured out into the world, I never wanted to face that again. I'm not cruel or evil, but loneliness is frightening, and I feel weak. My father tells me the opposite; he says I'm different, that I have a spiritual power inside me, which has given me strength since I was little.

I smiled and said, "He told me about that strange experience you had when you memorized some Quranic verses by heart."

"Did you believe that?"

"Why not?"

"For me, I don't recall it. My dad always tells that story, but I'm not perfect, and I don't want to be. I just want to be myself, nothing more."

"And I don't want anything more from you."

"So don't expect me to be like Rose. Rose built a whole world inside her cocoon and lived happily in it. I can't do the same, I would die."

"No harm will come to you with me by your side; rest assured."

"You told me that before. But you're gone. I dreamed many times that we were standing together on a high peak on the edge of a bottomless abyss, and I always jumped carelessly because I was holding your hand. Suddenly, you let go of my hand and disappeared. My ribs shattered, and the pieces of my dreams fell apart. The Lamees you knew died. Today I feel stupid just sitting with you. Let alone loving you again, you're putting me on a new peak and asking me to jump".

"I know I made a mistake, yet you should know that your love drove me away in the past. It was a new experience, and I was afraid of you. I was so in love with you that I lost myself in you. I didn't recognize myself, and I lost my identity in you. And you know what's funny?"

"What?"

"That, twenty years later, I still haven't regained my identity. I couldn't separate myself from you. You're still inside me, and I couldn't, and don't want to, rip you out of my chest. You have to trust that I won't let you down anymore. But the question is, do you still love me?"

"The trouble is that I find myself foolish and again ready to jump into the abyss. I think that's what's bothering me, making me lose my mind... I'm so scared."

"Don't be afraid anymore, I won't ever leave you now."

"Before you reappeared, my life was clear, at least. I knew what I wanted from men and understood what men wanted from me. My path was straightforward, but I lost myself and my equilibrium with you. That's what makes me angry—angry at myself."

"Why?"

"Because I hate to love you."

"You're confusing me."

"You bring me back to the cell I spent my life trying to escape from. But I discovered that the more I tried to forget and get away from you, the more attached I became to you. I'm now sure I'm addicted to you. I keep thinking about you; whenever I dream, I find myself in your arms. You have to love me or I'll go crazy."

She was talking with tears streaming down her cheeks. I laughed and told her:

"I will make you go crazy with my love."

"So shall we start over?" She said with a sweet smile.

" Ok, but before that, I owe you a debt you haven't fulfilled."

"What is it?"

"Do you remember what you said to me in that café in Nice? You said you wanted me. Since then, I promised to see the stars with you at noon."

She smiled shyly and said:

"You will see them with me tomorrow at dinner at my apartment."

Chapter Twenty-Four

Pleasure usually ends with orgasm for the woman and ejaculation for the man. The volcano of excitement subsides, the tension dissipates, and the soul calms down. But it's never over because the excitement comes back and reignites again, over and over again, endlessly, and each time we struggle to push the boulder to the top only to have it roll back down again. I always wonder what lies behind a man's attempt to make himself into a woman. Is it a desperate attempt to unite with her? To go back to the first point? The starting point? Couldn't that be how we try to bring things back to their beginnings? But at the same time, couldn't ejaculation be the process by which nature thwarts this attempt? What if something happened, a surprise, and nature fails to quell the body's revolution? In other words, what if we reach climax without ejaculation or orgasm?

The next day, the day that Lamees and I had agreed to meet, just one day before François left for Paris, we went with him to visit Rose and Ahmed's graves for the last time before traveling.

The sun was just about to set when I spotted Lamees, not dressed in black, outside the cemetery fence. She wore a colorful, loose-fitting dress that flowed gracefully over her body, enhancing her femininity. I was surprised when she showed up unexpectedly, her face illuminated by a bright smile. She gestured to me, and I walked over to her. I asked, astonished:

"What brings you here now? Isn't our date at your apartment tonight?"

She looked at me for a long time without answering, as if she were seeing me for the first time. There was something new and unfamiliar in her gaze. She said with a smile:

"I couldn't wait. I wanted to be near you."

The smell of her perfume was too much for me. I apologized to my sister and François and asked them to go home without me.

I went back to Lamees and was glad she came early. "Now, where do you like to go? "I said joyfully

"To Bab Srijeh." She said without hesitation

Her answer surprised me.

"Why? What's there?"

"You always say the answer to the mystery is there. I want to see what's there, so take us to Bab Srijeh."

I couldn't refuse her, especially with her squeezing my arm and looking at me with eyes dripping with lust.

"And then we'll go to your apartment like we agreed?"

"Then we go wherever you want us to go."

She had come without her car, so we took a taxi. I told the driver, "We want you to take us to Bab Srijeh." The driver looked around, gave me a strange look, and drove off."

I noticed the driver was giving me strange looks while I was busy talking to Lamees the entire way.

When we exited the car at the entrance to the souq, the driver kept looking at me strangely even as he drove away.

"Did you notice how the driver was looking at us?"

"Normally, I must have impressed him."

"But he was staring at me, not you."

Lamees smiled and didn't comment. She didn't seem as interested in the souq as she suggested; nothing caught her attention, and she wasn't looking at anything. Instead, she mostly looked at me, observing my hand movements while I explained some of the souk's features to her. Her behavior indicated that she already knew everything I was saying.

The souq was nearly empty, and most of the shops were closed. I told her there was nothing to see in the souq now that the shops were shut.

She said: "It's okay, it's enough for me to walk here and breathe in the smell of the place. I belong here."

"If you know the place so well, why did you bring us here?"

"I want you to take me to where the riddle is," I said skeptically. "I don't want to disappoint you, but I'm not sure it's still a mystery. Almost everyone agrees that it was just an..." illusion.

"Still, take us there."

"A few days ago, we were there, François and I, and there was nothing."

She said firmly

"I said, take us there."

"OK, OK, why are you being so stubborn?"

As we approached the narrow lane, a sense of dread washed over me. I felt uneasy about going back, especially since the souq was starting to darken.

But when we got there and stood at the alley entrance, I felt there was no reason for all that fear. When I looked inside, I didn't find the dread I felt when I came two days ago. It was brightly lit and more colorful than the last time. People were walking around normally.

I said, "Here is the mysterious alley."

"Let's go inside,' she said, clinging to me."

I thought she was scared, I said: We can go back, but she said with determination: "No, let's go in, I don't see anything to be afraid of. It's a normal lane."

Though it was very narrow, men and women walked by, children played, and there was nothing unusual about it.

At one of the turns, there was a large, old, and traditional building with a lit entrance, from which you could hear the sounds of laughter and music, and vapor rising, giving the alley a magical, foggy atmosphere. Lamees asked me: "What's here?"

"I don't know, we didn't notice this building when we came last time. It looks like a hammam (public bath).

It was indeed a traditional hammam.

A hostess stood at the entrance, smiled affectionately, and invited us in.

Lamees said, "Let's go in and explore."

"But it's a hammam, what will we do?"

"We take a bath." she said, laughing. "Come on, come on."

She grabbed me by the hand and we went in.

There was a receptionist. She asked us with a smile: "Do you want to take a bath?"

Lamees said immediately: "Yes."

"Is this your first time here?"

"Yes."

"Well, we will give you a private suite for comfort and privacy. Come with me."

All the staff working in the hammam were women. They toiled diligently, moving like butterflies around the space, carrying towels and toiletries to various locked rooms. The scent of soap and perfume rising with the steam was relaxing and comforting:

"What a wonderful place! I said, " How did we not discover it before? It's beautiful and the service is excellent."

The hostess opened a closed door for us and let us in. The place was a large hall, with curtains covering the walls and candles in every corner. In the center was a pool of water with roses floating on its surface and vapors rising from it, carrying a fragrant scent. Dreamy, soothing music floated through the space, and pillows and cushions surrounded us. I stood there, looking around in awe. Lamees held my forearm and squeezed it joyfully. I felt relaxed, calm, and peaceful.

The hostess said, "You will find everything you need here, and no one will disturb you." Then she smiled and said as she stood at the door: "I hope you have a nice bath."

I looked at my watch and asked her: "What time does the Hammam close? "

"Don't worry, sir, we never close, don't let time distract you from enjoying your bath."

The stewardess left us and closed the door behind her.

"What a beautiful place!" I said to Lamees

She didn't comment and just smiled. I approached her, took her hand, and said: "Close your eyes: Close your eyes."

She smiled and closed her eyes. I took the watch out of my pocket. I put it around her wrist.

As soon as she saw it, she gasped and couldn't stifle a scream of joy. She looked at it with a strange glint in her eye.

"I want you to keep it. Look inside; this is my red heart. It says Lamees with every tick of its hands."

She was so happy that she cried with tears

"It's gorgeous, thank you."

I didn't expect her to be so happy about it; it's just a watch. I approached the pool and put my hand in the water to check its temperature. It felt warm and inviting. I turned to Lamees, and she was naked, smiling at me as she stepped into the water. She held out her hand to me, and I quickly undressed and followed her in.

Lamees was different. There was a magic about her. She had never been more beautiful or sexy before that night. The lust in her eyes was unbridled. My dream was finally going to come true. Lamees was everything I wanted in a woman and more. She was everything I dreamed of in sex and more. It was enough for my fingers to touch her body to ignite the desire to burn and set the fire of lust within me. She responded to my desires as I would like her to and reacted as I would like her to. There was harmony and music between us in every movement, every touch, and every kiss. I reached the peak of my lust, but couldn't ejaculate, and she was writhing in pleasure in my arms, completely surrendering to me. I kept pushing myself into her, pushing and pushing and pushing like I was trying to catch a train that was constantly moving away from me. My lust doesn't subside, it only intensifies, and I keep pushing, and she digs her nails into my skin and bites my shoulder with her teeth.

Suddenly, I felt a flash of light inside my head, like a spark of lightning from inside my brain, a flash that carried with it a tremendous pleasure that ran through my entire body, greater than any ejaculation. I closed my eyes in ecstasy and felt my body floating in space.

My mind was not as clear as it used to be, and many thoughts and images ran through it. I heard Lamees's voice saying, "How does it feel, Mamdouh?"

I was surprised that I wasn't Mamdouh.

I said, "Who is Mamdouh?"

She asked me: "Who are you then? I said, "I am Ahmed."

She said: "And who am I?" I looked at her. She was Rose.

I thought again. How did this happen? I was Mamdouh, but now I am Ahmed, and all of Ahmed's memories, emotions, and sensations are inside me. I am Ahmed, and I have so much lust and love for Rose. The lust in me was still raging, and Rose or Lamees was still in my lap, and I was still pushing myself into her, but I couldn't ejaculate. Suddenly, there was a second flash, and the pleasure flowed through my being again, and I was no longer my own. I became bigger than myself. I now had my grandfather's memory; Ahmed was my son, and Mamdouh was my grandson. The flashes continued until my being was flooded with a tremendous light. I became like a beam traveling in the opposite direction, returning to its starting point. During this return journey, it collects within itself the entire memory of the universe. With each memory, my pleasure grew and demanded more. I carried the memory of my grandparents and great-grandparents. I stored the memory of scientists, writers, philosophers, and thinkers within me. Everything in the universe seemed insignificant in front of this tremendous amount of consciousness, and I wasn't sure if it was coming out of me or into me. I was inhaling without exhaling. Every time my chest filled with air, it asked for more.

I hugged her tighter and said frantically: "I want more." I was moving toward the beginning, toward that little dot, toward the greater mystery.

I squeezed her in my arms:

"I want more, I want to get there. The light is intense and dazzling, but it doesn't hurt my eyes, because I was seeing without eyes and swimming without a body."

But Suddenly

Suddenly, the phone rang.

Suddenly, the world went dark.

The phone kept ringing; it didn't stop. It kept ringing. I wanted it to stop, but it kept pounding on my head. I felt myself falling and falling, and I found myself hitting the ground. I opened my eyes but couldn't see anything; it was pitch black, and I couldn't see anything around me.

As my eyes adjusted to the darkness, I found myself sitting in the narrow alley of that deserted neighborhood, alone and naked; the phone kept ringing. I was lost in thought, the fog in my mind paralyzing my ability to think. It was Lamees' voice on the other end.

"Mamdouh? Where are you, Mamdouh?

"I'm here .... No, I'm there."

"Mamdouh, I'm Lamees. What's going on with you?

"You're Lamees? But Lamees is here. I gave her the watch".

"What are you saying? What watch?"

"Rose is here too."

"You're scaring me. Tell me, where are you?"

"I'm in Bab Srijeh, no, I'm everywhere."

"Calm down and tell me what happened."

I growled, "Why are you bothering me? What is it that you want from me?"

She was taken aback by my anger and asked me fearfully:

"What's wrong with you, Mamdouh? Did you forget our date tonight at my apartment?"

But I didn't pay attention to her question, I ignored it and asked her:

"Do you know who I am, Lamees?"

"Damn it Mamdouh, what kind of question is that?"

I ignored her again and answered my own question: "I am Mamdouh, but do you know who else I am?"

Lamees started crying on the other end, crying in despair:

"Don't leave me, Mamdouh, please, what's wrong with you?"

I continued with a thick fog clouding my eyes:

"I'm also my father. Yes, I'm Ahmed; I'm my grandfather. I'm all of them, and all of them are me."

I was there, Lamees …

I was the universe and the universe was me …

It was me, because….

In the beginning … I was there … in the beginning was…. I.

Mahmoud Farra
2025/06/03

www.ingramcontent.com/pod-product-compliance
Lightning Source LLC
Chambersburg PA
CBHW070325010526
44107CB00004B/411